From David
1988

DEAD AS DOORNAILS

Anthony Cronin

Dead as Doornails

a chronicle of life

The Dolmen Press Dublin
London: Calder & Boyars

Set in Bembo type and printed in the Republic of Ireland
by the Richview Press
for The Dolmen Press Limited
North Richmond Street Dublin 1
Published in association with The Talbot Press Limited
Spring 1976

ISBN 0 85105 304 1
THE DOLMEN PRESS

ISBN 0 7145 109 20
CALDER & BOYARS

Acknowledgement is made to the National Gallery of Ireland for permission to reproduce the portraits of Brendan Behan on p. 37, Patrick Kavanagh on p. 77, and Brian O'Nolan (Myles na Gopaleen) on p. 113.

Cover photograph: Mateo Terrades Miklankova
Collection Anthony Kerrigan, Palma de Mallorca

for
Bob and Sheila Bradshaw

Although this is a narrative, it is not an autobiography, except in so far as all the seven men remembered in it played some part in my life and are seen through my eyes. There is no significance in the number chosen, outside the fact that they are all dead; they all died within a short space of time of each other; all of them were acquainted with some of the others; and I was acquainted with them all.

A.C.

1

MY SUBJECT is not myself and my doings, but it is never any harm to establish a little circumstance. In 1948 I had ceased to be a student and had become, for some reason, a barrister-at-law. It was a state in which I took no pride; indeed I was acutely ashamed of it for a number of reasons, some of them ideological and connected with whatever amalgam of anarchism and utopian communism I luxuriated in at the time, some to do with the fact that I was a poet, in so far as I was anything that could be named, and thought the barristership consorted ill with the practice of the art and the necessary dooms that attached to the calling. I was too ignorant to know that Beaumont and Fletcher, Browne of Tavistock, John Donne, Patrick Pearse, William Cowper, W. S. Gilbert, Sir Walter Scott and Robert Louis Stevenson, among others, had been in the same boat.

But in any case the company and general demeanour of my contemporaries who were now repairing to the Bar library, that peculiar communal place of business in the Four Courts, did not appeal to me. Among them I experienced what I think is probably a not uncommon mixture of feelings: superiority and inferiority at the same time, the latter for certain social reasons, ludicrous in the retrospect and impossible now to define, and by this time I felt, and I dare say looked, an oddity. Besides, I had never had any intention of practising the profession, though since I have never been any good at long-term decisions, nor very much aware of what I really want beyond certain fundamentals, I had never thought about the matter very clearly. Drift had, up to now, been the order of the day.

So I got a job—ideologically of course as indefensible as

the practice of law—in the offices of an association of retail traders, bluffing my way through a large field of candidates with the aid of the barristership and some borrowed clothes, the only use the former had ever been to me, if it was a use. The job was supposed to be a bit of a prize—other members of the senior branch of the legal profession had applied. But then, hard times were in it all round. The facts were that I earned seven pounds three shillings a week, paid three pounds for digs and drank the rest. The borrowed clothes had been returned. My own were in no sort of shape. I was no good at the job. I was not happy and I knew it.

My personal inadequacies and griefs were many. There was my relationship with my parents and theirs with the onset of age; my non-existent sex life, perhaps really an improvement over student dating and courting, though that was not how I saw the lack; my sufferings in the office. But anyway Dublin in the late nineteen-forties was an odd and, in many respects, unhappy place. The malaise that seems to have affected everywhere in the aftermath of war took strange forms there, perhaps for the reason that the war itself had been a sort of ghastly unreality. Neutrality had left a wound, set up complexes in many, including myself, which the post-war did little to cure.

Nor were there then concourses of young poets to associate with, such as exist to keep each other company to-day. Most of the elder ones, known to local fame, were respectable Gaelic revivalists, in orthodox employment in the civil service or the radio station. Left becalmed in the wake of genius, they sat, it seemed, nightly in the Pearl or the Palace, comforting themselves with large whiskeys, reminiscences of F. R. Higgins and discussions of assonance, before going home to the suburbs. One recognised their life-style as the *vie lettres* locally accepted and approved. It was not somehow attractive, nor probably attainable, but of course one felt the lack of confreres. Except for one or two who had been student poets along with me, and were now busy bracing themselves for the serious business of getting on in the world, I had none. I disliked, as I say, my childish, snobbish, bar contemporaries. I knew no girls; could not be bothered to go through the motions necessary

2

to pick one sort up in dancehalls, nor make the arrangements involved in taking another to the middle-class dress and supper dances in the Gresham and the Metropole which appeared to provide my contemporaries with a large part of their social and, such as it was, their sex life. What I needed, I obscurely felt, was a bohemia of some kind, but I did not know where to find one.

Then things suddenly took a turn for the better. I got thrown out of digs and met an acquaintance to whom I explained my problem, which was really that I could not afford ordinary digs and do my drinking at the same time. He told me he knew about a place where I might get to stay pretty cheaply and told me the name of the pub where I might find the owner. The pub was McDaid's; and the place was the since-famous Catacombs. I did not know it then, but my feet had been happily set upon the downward path, and there was to be no looking back.

McDaid's is in Harry Street, off Grafton Street, Dublin's main boulevard of chance and converse. It has an extraordinarily high ceiling and high, almost Gothic, windows in the front wall, with stained glass borders. The general effect is church-like or tomb-like, according to mood: indeed indigenous folk-lore has it that it once was a meeting-house for a resurrection sect who liked high ceilings in their places of resort because the best thing of all would be for the end of the world to come during religious service and in that case you would need room to get up steam.

The type of customer who awaited the resurrection and the life to come has varied a little over the years, but in spite of rather weak-minded attempts to make it so, McDaid's was never merely a literary pub. Its strength was always in variety, of talent, class, caste and estate. The divisions between writer and non-writer, bohemian and artist, informer and revolutionary, male and female, were never rigorously enforced; and nearly everybody, gurriers included, was ready for elevation, to Parnassus, the scaffold or wherever.

At the time of which I speak the company was very various. There was a number of painters and sculptors, few of them serious, fewer to last. There were some Americans, ex-servicemen who had come to Ireland originally to be

Trinity students under the G.I. Bill and remained on when its bounty was exhausted, among them J. P. Donleavy, then supposed to be a painter but meditating a big book about Ireland to be called, I seem to remember, 'Under The Stone'; and Gainor Crist, who was to provide the original for that book, subsequently *The Ginger Man* (a curiously transformed and lessened portrait) and to die, in appalling circumstances, in the Canary Islands in the early sixties.

Originally perhaps because of the association of Desmond MacNamara, a sculptor who had a studio nearby, with the late 'Pope' O'Mahoney and the Republican Prisoners' Aid Fund, there were numbers of former prisoners, variously in need of aid of diverse kinds (some of it highly unorthodox) and fairly recently released from various gaols and internment camps in Britain and Ireland. In fact if the prevailing atmosphere in McDaid's at this time could have been described, bohemian-revolutionary might have been the phrase. Eddie Connell, who had been, in I.R.A. parlance, 'Officer Commanding Portland, Isle of Wight', and Peter Walsh, who had similarly 'commanded' the I.R.A. prisoners in Dartmoor, were prominent; but there were many others, chiefly ex-internees from the Irish government's camp at the Curragh; and, to go with them, in case there were any lingering vestiges of activism about, there were a few special branch men, or reputed special branch men. Not many of the I.R.A. had orthodox, or indeed any, employment, no more than had the sprinkling of latter-day anarchists, communists etc. who had followed them in, or the bohemian *rentiers*, many of them English or very Anglo-Irish, who rejoiced in the general atmosphere. There were also a few girls, some of whom had employment as wives, mistresses or otherwise, some not.

Most of this company assembled in McDaid's every day under the benevolent aegis of one of the great barmen of all time, Paddy O'Brien, and almost every night the entire assemblage moved on to the Catacombs. These and what went on there have been described so often now, in works of apparent fiction like *The Ginger Man*, or alleged fact such as Mr. Ulick O'Connor's biography of Brendan Behan, that another description may seem, as they say, superfluous. But still . . .

The Catacombs had once been the basement, composed of kitchen, pantries and wine-cellar, with presumably also a servant's bedroom or two and their attendant corridors, of one of those high Georgian mansions that are the pride of Dublin. One went down the area steps and through a pantry into the kitchen, which was large, low-ceilinged and vaulted, with a flagged floor. The whole place smelt of damp, decaying plaster and brickwork, that smell of money gone which was once so prevalent in Ireland. Off the corridor leading out of the kitchen were various dark little rooms. Mine had, I think, once been the wine-cellar. There was hardly space for a bed in it, and none for anything else except a few bottles and books.

The other rooms were variously occupied and people came and went according to need and circumstance, but our host was a great stickler for the rent, so one had to preserve some sort of affluence or go. There was never any difficulty about gatherings, however, for he lived partly on the proceeds of the bottles that the revellers brought and left behind. He was rumoured by outsiders—who rumoured much in those days about both McDaid's and the Catacombs —to have another source of income; but, although once in the watches of the night I heard him ejecting some young lout who had apparently accompanied him home under a misapprehension with the angry declaration that he was not accustomed to pay but to be paid for whatever it was, as far as my observation went anyway the charge was unfounded, and what he was saying was a mere boast.

Ireland has changed somewhat since, and I suppose the existence of our little enclave had something to do with the change, but so holy was Ireland then and so strangely afraid that I still hear lurid descriptions of our goings on, descriptions echoed with a delightful innocence recently in Mr. Ulick O'Connor's book. Alas, no. When asked, '*Qu'as tu fait de ta jeunesse?*' I can truthfully answer: 'Even with this part of it, not enough, not nearly enough.'

Most of what went on in the Catacombs was in fact ordinary social boozing. Where there is booze, it will usually prevail over other matters. The Irish for a musical gathering, a concert, is *cuirm cheoil,* the combination of words indicating a necessary connection between song and drink. That is what we had in the Catacombs. Nearly every regular frequenter had a party piece. One had thousands. This was Brendan Behan.

When I first went to McDaid's and took up residence in the Catacombs, Brendan was in Paris, whither he had gone with Gainor Crist and a Limerick man who had come into a small legacy and was disposed to spend it, if such can be imagined. His doings there were much storied and talked about and his return was much heralded. It was a wet Sunday morning when he eventually arrived in the pub. He had his father, mother and brothers with him and there was a large company assembled, but as we walked up Leeson Street towards the Catacombs at three o'clock closing, he fell back deliberately so that we walked together. Friendship, like other forms of love, takes immediately or not at all. In the course of that otherwise dismal Sunday afternoon we became friends and discovered we were confreres.

Brendan in those days was far from being the gross ogre whose picture became so familiar years later in the English newspapers. He was fat, it is true, for his height and age, but his girth combined with his personality gave the impression that he was somehow merely bursting at the seams. Nor was the porcine effect, to be produced later on by the contrast between his general grossness and his tiny hands and feet, apparent: one was struck instead by the sort of expansive and inflationary possibilities he managed to extract from the contrast, like an operatic tenor who can seemingly expand parts of his anatomy at will.

At this time he worked, when it suited him, and when he was not on his travels, at the house-painting which was his father's trade, but he had published a few poems in Irish and a documentary piece about one of his terms of imprisonment in *The Bell*—he belonged, he said, to 'that large and respectable body in the community that had once had an article in that magazine'. Both then and later he would pose when it suited him as much more of an orthodox working-class product than he really was. In fact there were currents of

6

literacy, liberalism and unconventionality on both sides of his family which many a product of the lower middle-classes like myself might have had cause to envy. And on one side there was a strong theatrical tradition. (His uncle was a music-hall song-writer who had written the national anthem.) If the realities of working-class life were known to him it was also true that he had never been among the great unacquainted submerged; there was plenty of acquaintance and tradition about in his growing-up; and indeed it was, to some extent at least, the show business element in him that contributed to his destruction in the end.

He lived for the most part in his parents' house, out in the grey spaces of Crumlin, a working-class housing estate dating from the 'thirties, better than some of the more recent experiments in ghettoisation, but not a very cheerful place all the same. However, he was nomadic by nature and it was frequently too far from him to go in the small hours, so he stayed wherever he was welcome, and often in the Cata-combs. Sometimes in the days to come he would share my palliasse in the wine-cellar and on these occasions we would talk long in the mornings, and then when the pubs were open venture forth into the streets, in search of company, drink and diversion. These days became more frequent as my resolution, such as it ever had been, weakened, my new acquaintance developed, and my hold on the job loosened in the clouds of hangover. Eventually I gave it up altogether and became fairly happily jobless, though beginning to publish poems and ill-informed critical comment in the backs of such magazines as there were.

You could not in fact have a better companion in a day's idleness than Brendan. He was a kaleidoscopic entertain-ment, but he was also fecund in serious ideas. He had a line in bemused wonderment about the activities of the world which was only partly an affectation, for he was genuinely naïve in certain ways and genuinely full of questionings. And he knew too when to drop the act and show himself capable of intimacy. The salt which makes penury palatable, ironic com-ment on all forms of possession and ownership, sometimes quite savage, he had in abundance. He had also in those days the remarkable gift of being able to realise and humorously illuminate the other person's circumstance while comically examining his own; and he was a good ally, fiercely contemptuous of all who disapproved of one's way of life. 'Fuck the begrudgers', he used to say, the implication being that envy lay at the root of most such disapproval.

He talked a lot in those days about his homosexuality, though I have since met others who knew him then and who claim they never heard of the matter. Mostly when he spoke of it, it was not as a difficulty but as a distinction. Sometimes he averted to it simply to shock. In the presence of a bishop and a curate for example, if that unlikely eventuality can be imagined, he would declare that he fancied the curate, or perhaps even the bishop, in order to shock the one and embarrass the other. He used to say wryly that De Valera's housing reforms had ruined his ordinary sexual development; that the move from the cosy slums out to the windy spaces and semi-detached houses of Crumlin had come at a crucial age and had been disastrous. On the landings and in the dark hallways of the tenements you could always get a grope or a squeeze and at fourteen he was just getting the hang of things and acquiring the necessary casualness of approach when the move came along, the casual courting opportunities among childhood acquaintances vanished and the elaborate approaches and settings-up which all sensitive, shy adolescents find difficult became the order of the day. This history was not advanced as a justification or a pathology nor, to do him credit, were his prison experiences. 'No worse than boarding school', he said he supposed, and in terms of my own experience, we agreed he was right.

It was agreed also that whatever the accidents or the latent tendencies involved one would probably have suffered in any case from the Irish syndrome. Apart altogether from prisons or boarding schools, 'life' would not have lived up to certain literary notions. 'Normal' adolescent development, 'normal' adolescent ecstasies were a myth. Something had gone wrong somewhere along the line, as it was pretty well bound to: though you could of course be cheerful about your flaws or your freedoms and suggest that it had gone right. This feeling was perhaps particularly strong in our generation. You could, and most people did, blame the

8

Catholic religion, of which, incidentally, in the early days—he was to become rather maudlin about the matter later—Brendan had a ferocious hatred. The war, with its impediments to ordinary living, had something to do with it. So had boarding schools. And prisons. Indeed perhaps government housing estates.

It is almost impossible for sensitive, intelligent, over-imaginative people not to make a hames of their development anyway and then only two responses are really open to them; they can believe themselves the ultimate oddity, or they can suggest that everybody else is lying. There are always those of course who lay claim both to sensitivity and simplicity of development; who allege that in spite or because of their poetic imaginations they slipped into life and cunts as to the manner born. Patrick Kavanagh was later to invent a word to cover this sort of literary pretence along with other related ones: 'bucklepping'. As far as we were concerned the buckleppers were liars.

In public Brendan's manner was rabelaisian, jocose, knowledgeable. In private he would admit to difficulties and bewilderments about which he was in fact much funnier. Unfortunately for him, his writing—with the possible exception of *Borstal Boy*—when he eventually got round to it, was a public matter also, and as a way of sorting himself out through the rigours, honesties and ironies of art, it was largely useless to him. That was part of the debacle.

Whatever the truth of his assertions about his basic homosexuality may have been, I do not ever remember him striking up any sort of a liaison, and though there were considerably less admitted homosexuals around in our age-group in those days, there were enough. Nor did he give any surface impression of being queer: of course, contrary to popular belief, most people who are do not: the word covers a multitude of sins and states anyway.

Apart from being queer, he claimed that he suffered from what he called 'a Herod complex', a preference for youth, named so after Herod's fancying the daughter rather than the mother. He fancied only boys of about fourteen to eighteen, he would say; and in the right circumstances these declarations were usually made publicly, humorously and loudly enough to destroy any prospect of success. Once when we were sharing the wine-cellar together he made advances to myself: perhaps he felt he had to. The matter being cheerfully disposed of was never heard of again, through all our wanderings and bunkings.

He complained, however, of strange ignorances and naïveties where 'ordinary' sex and the female were concerned; and was bitter about those who, not being privy to his real preferences, prescribed more orthodox sex as a corrective to our way of life. When reproached once by a progressive lady we knew for not having a regular girl-friend, Brendan replied that it was every bit as un-Marxist to reproach a man for not having a fancy woman as it would be to reproach him for not having a motor-car. For a long time afterwards he used to refer to her suggestion that all his ills and malaises would disappear if he had more sex as 'Dr. so-and-so's remedy for the human condition'.

But even about the physical side of homosexual relationships he would admit to bewilderments. He came across something in Enid Starkie's biography of Rimbaud which apparently bothered him and led to much speculation; and he spent days in the National Library reading various accounts of the trial of Oscar Wilde to find out precisely what practices Oscar had engaged in—the only time I can remember him ever going near the place.

In saying all this I do not mean to suggest that Brendan was more than ordinarily ignorant, naïve or innocent about sex. Quite the contrary in fact. And if one were to take some of his boastings for gospel one would have to assume heights—or depths—of sophistication rather rare at the time. These boastings were not of the ordinary kind, however, suggesting mere conquest and procured licence. There was in them an element of picaresque braggadocio which was meant to suggest cynicism and villainy on his part. He did, at one time, have a penchant for such boastings and surprised me by asserting that he got money from a woman I knew for performing what was to him a particularly onerous, not to say unpleasant, sexual service for her.

However that may be, and behind all the boastings and the jokes, what is certain to me is this: Brendan, when I knew him first, had a much more complex awareness of himself, his diffidences, failures and complications than he chose to present even then, and more especially later, to the outside world. He knew he was complicated and he chose to deal with the complications in the best way possible: ironic confession, humorous self-disparagement, mock surprise, combined of course with a satiric savagery about the pretensions of other people. Unfortunately very little of this appears later on in his work or his alleged work, whichever it happens to be. Here the complications and their confessional shadows are constantly at the mercy of bravado, show, pretence. And in the public figure as well as in the writer, for the two are now inseparable, it is the same. He is the great liver, who has drunk it to the lees at all stages of the game, the great avatar of booze and sex and 'life'. Fatal of course, the more so because part of our nature impels us to try 'to become what we sing'; even though, the more our pretences take over, the more we secretly know how much we need 'the deep counter-minings of art'.

In public, comic drama was Brendan's primary mode of being and his enormous talent for it was constantly employed in enactments of one kind or another, created anywhere there was an audience, from the cold morning kitchen of the Catacombs to the partially empty McDaid's of the mid-afternoon. Some of these were merely satirical in intent and involved imaginary scenes between people we knew; but he had too a strangely coherent if very mixed mythology, peopled by miscellaneous patriotic and literary figures, and in the miniature dramas involving these an extraordinary talent for the grotesque took over, so that the originals attained a new surrealist dimension.

'The childhood of D. H. Lawrence' was a very elaborate performance, often repeated with many variations, in which Lawrence's drunken father comes home to find the boy reading a book and keeps up a running stream of monstrous abuse of the child while getting into the bath and having his back scrubbed, Brendan playing scurrilous father, anxious mother and patronising little boy in various postures and with accents varying from broad Yorkshire to badly culti-vated middle-class English. 'The boyhood of John Ruskin' was created as a sort of companion piece one winter night in the Catacombs when there was very little to drink, and it took the sensitive Ruskin and his doting parents on a tour of Europe in which sulkings and reconciliations, aesthetic wonderments, raptures and incomprehensions alternated. How Ruskin came to find a place in his mythology I do not know, but his reading, being a matter of chance, was strangely various. 'Maud Gonne at the Microphone' was usually performed with a towel over the head by way of a veil and it consisted of fruity recollections of Yeats in a quavering, aged, but, of certain undertones, deeply expressive voice. 'Mr Cosgrave's Visit to Mountjoy' involved the former President of the Free State in a scene with a patriotic lady who to her chagrin is not arrested in a general swoop. She puts a camp bed outside the gates of the prison, gets into it and goes on hunger strike. Goaded by questions in the Dail about the ill-treatment of other republican lady prisoners who are on hunger strike within, Mr Cosgrave arrives at the prison in a motor-car to see for himself. The disappointed lady rises up in her camp bed and calls after him : 'Imperalist! Lackey! West Briton! Liar! Arrest me! Arrest me!' To which Mr Cosgrave turns round and replies: 'Madame. Imperialist I may be. Lackey I may be. Liar I may even be. But I am not a collector of curiosities.' The rich part of the performance consisted of the lady attiring herself suitably for her vigil, setting up the camp bed, composing herself on it, and refusing all offers of refreshment.

These vignettes were, where possible, embellished and illustrated by song; but he loved song anyway and was happy to sing anywhere and in almost any circumstance. He had a resonant baritone, perfect pitch, and, again, an enormous theatrical sense, whether for the rendition of scurrilous comic pieces or passionate patriotic and left-wing ballads— often the two merged into one. According to what was needed by the song, the lips would curl, the eyes flash and roll and the tiny, sensitive hands clench or unclench in passion, or reach out in mock unavailing yearning and despair.

It was, in all its elements, an original form of *cabaret intime* and it was a highly developed art. Given the proper circumstances he might have used it to feed the exhibitionist in himself that eventually devoured him and the unsatisfied actor who interrupted his own plays, desperate to appear on stage himself and be, for every moment of the performance, the centre of love and attention. It was not an ignoble art—far from it. It was spontaneous, and as his later addiction to the tape-recorder apart from anything else shows, he was an essentially spontaneous creator, who needed company in the act. It drew from its audience and depended on a confidence in affection given and received which might have been the ultimate reassurance for one who so feared to go it alone. It might certainly, ephemeral or otherwise, have been a better outlet for him than the tape-recorder. Perhaps there was a better, and certainly a happier artist of another kind lost in Brendan.

2

TIME PASSED. Brendan and I spent some of it out in Ralph Cusack's house in County Wicklow. It stood on the side of a hill which sloped down to the upper waters of the Avoca River and on the opposite hillside was a wood which flamed and died unforgettably that autumn. 'Is it any wonder I can't paint any longer?' cried Ralph to me, tears streaming down his cheeks as we stood in the doorway. After a young manhood spent on the Continent, principally the Riviera of the thirties, he had come back to Ireland during the war and bought a house in the Wicklow mountains. He had always been supposed to be a painter—in his sort of intellectual-rentier bohemia you had to be something. Ireland in those years was the haunt of many refugee non-combatants, sensitives and progressives of one kind or another. There was accordingly much artistic activity, but standards were not high and so Ralph flourished for a while in this new oasis. Alas, even so, although others might be convinced or might pretend to be, he knew himself that the paintings, of which there were dozens in the room upstairs where I slept, were terrible. Apocalyptic nightmare forms whirled, intersected, balanced and collapsed, tired by their own pretence of energy, that most enervating pretence of all. Cones penetrated ovoids to no purpose. The brush was heavy, the spirit weak. But what is one to do when one has a certain amount of money, is an immensely civilised and intelligent man and rejects religion, 'a career' and the bourgeois conventions? Surely art is the answer?

Later he was to emigrate to the South of France, grow acres of roses for a living and write a moderately celebrated book, *Cadenze,* which largely fails to contain his personality.

It is a failure analogous to Brendan's and yet different, for Ralph had spent his young manhood believing in the sub-conscious and when he came to write he insisted on digging deep into it. Unfortunately the sub-conscious in his case, as in that of many other left-wing surrealists, including the French whom he so admired, turned out to be inhabited not by truths but by mere wishes, so that his book is a sort of pretentious schoolboy fantasy with heavy psychological–environmental–consequential themes. Instead of letting himself emerge from a funny account of doings and disgraces in his past, he had to show his hero as a significant, if comic, product of his upbringing and environment. As Kavanagh was to put it: 'He doesn't realise how amusing he really is. He thought he had to psycho-analyse and be interesting.'

Amusing, and more, he certainly was. I first arrived out in his house one night with Brendan, a painter acquaintance of those days, and his girl friend. On the night of our arrival we all sat round the kitchen table after supper, drinking. Although we had not been expected, there was certainly enough drink in the house to float a battleship. Ralph seemingly admired our painter friend and he had recently read a poem of mine in a magazine. He accordingly thanked Brendan with tears in his eyes 'for bringing to my house the two young artists in Ireland I most wanted to meet'. Whether or not it was meant, it was said; and I was new to the sort of household where art was taken with any sort of seriousness. Certainly there were none among the Irish middle-classes. Ralph's household seemed to me then to be one of the most civilised I had ever been in; and, in spite of the scenes I was subsequently to witness as that extraordinary man thrashed around among his yearnings, enthusiasms and despairs, by and large it does still.

When I knew Patrick Kavanagh later on he was to describe Ralph to me as 'the arch phony'. I don't want to go ahead of my story, so suffice it to say here that according to Kavanagh's oft-repeated opinion any artist or would-be artist with a private income, especially from Anglo-Irish sources and Ralph's grandfather had been a titled gentleman and a principal shareholder in the Great Southern Railway—was a 'phony'. The existence of such people 'confused the issue', distracted attention from 'the genuine article', weakened his position if only because numbers are never an advantage to him, as in the case of the 'standing army of Irish poets' which amounted to twenty thousand when the bardic order assembled at Druim Ceat 'and has never been allowed to fall below that figure'. Such people were also inclined to be mean under pressure and to suggest to the sufferer that they, being artists themselves, are exempt from the small tolls he is of necessity compelled to levy on his richer acquaintance. 'They fear', he would say, 'that no-one will love them for their art alone and not their yellow gold'. As for their desperation, he admitted it and pitied them for it, but 'art could be no man's salvation except the artist's'; they confused art with self-expression, which it wasn't; and 'the king you seek you must bring with you'. Besides, he 'found it hard to like anybody richer than myself'.

Anyway, as we sat around the kitchen table, I remarked to myself on the level of civilisation obtaining, warmed as we were on a cold Autumn night by the Esse cooker inseparable from the kitchens of Irish country houses, the whiskey, the converse and a very genuine sort of affection that Ralph himself could radiate. A moment later it seemed that civilisation was about to break down.

Brendan had disappeared for quite a long time and Ralph's eldest boy, then about fourteen, who had been in and about while we talked, was absent along with him, until he reappeared alone, with tears on his face and unable or unwilling to say what had happened. We all, I think, leaped to the same conclusion, and I must say I was shocked, both because of the circumstances, 'under a man's own roof etc.', and because, in spite of his verbal exhibitionism, to have actually made a pass at such a boy at such an age seemed so extraordinarily unlike Brendan. Yet, there stood the boy, now weeping again and resistant to questions, and there in a moment stood Brendan himself, looking remarkably hangdog.

Ralph stood up. He was a short but barrel-chested man, with broad shoulders and long arms. In spite of Brendan's chat on the bus coming out I did not know then about his bouts of violence, but even the most peaceable of fathers might incline to murder in the circumstances. 'Brendan', he said softly, 'Have you . . .?'

'I swear to God, Ralph . . .' said Brendan.

'Roy,' said Ralph, 'has Brendan . . .?'

The boy shook his head, sobbing still. What he thought was meant I do not know.

'I swear to God, Ralph', said Brendan again, and in view of what I now know the form of words is ironic, 'I swear to God I didn't touch him'.

Perhaps because it was now said, and it carried such assurance, Ralph sat down; his wife took the boy, who was the son of a previous marriage, from the kitchen; and after some awkwardnesses, we all got back into our stride.

Much later I learned what did happen. Apparently Brendan had found the boy in the music room, as it was called, and he had got into that sort of matey, comradely, questioning converse with him that some men and many drunks adopt with boys, whether sexually attracted to them or not, patronisingly indulging—perhaps unconsciously—in a display of their superior life-wisdom and experience. The discussion had ranged wide, and the boy, who, in spite of his parents' beliefs, attended a Quaker school—there was of course a shortage of agnostic progressive schools in Ireland—confessed, not only to a belief in God, but to the kind of intense love of him that some people feel in adolescence and perhaps never again. Brendan, whom he admired very much, retorted with a savage attack on the concept of deity, calling to his aid all the stock arguments there are, and perhaps, being carried away by drink and that hatred of all forms of religion, especially the Catholic Church, which was in those days one of his strongest traits, giving them an even more than usually scurrilous point and edge. The boy fled, distressed by conflicting loyalties, wept by himself in the dark corridor, and came into the kitchen showing signs of having done so.

Here the grotesque part of it started. Ralph, the product of his time and generation, marred almost irretrievably as he felt he had been by a Church of Ireland and English public school upbringing, hated the concept of the deity too, and the boy had kept his devotion and love a secret. In the kitchen he could not or would not or was afraid to say what had happened. Meanwhile, all of us, having heard Brendan on the subject of his penchant for adolescents, of course believed the worst. Ralph was officially a raging liberal, but even liberals are inclined to get angry when they believe their young sons are being led down sexual by-ways, and, perhaps, even among liberals, the wolf should not cry wolf about himself too often.

In any case the liberal ethic, though, officially at least, it ruled Ralph's hospitable household as the teachings of Cornelius Jansen once ruled Port Royal, had, as I was to find out, its weaknesses. Though fanatically devoted to all the good, left-wing, liberal causes; hating censorship, obscurantism, prejudice, puritanism, occidental religions of all descriptions (oriental ones were of course another matter) as he did; prepared as he was to assert the absolute right of all men and women to all forms of behaviour which did not conflict with the rights of others; pacifist, humanitarian, sedulously progressive as he remained; he was extraordinarily prone to violence as an answer to what he believed or imagined to be defiance or contradiction of his principles.

As I am to relate, I became a resident in the house, and many's the man I saw battered to the ground or forced to flee into the night and walk the twenty-odd miles across Calary bog back to Dublin because he had offended, either in actual fact or in Ralph's sometimes fevered imagination, against the principles that were dear to his pacifist and un-prejudiced heart. Thus on one particularly awful evening, when there was a large gathering present, Brendan was assaulted with a bottle because he had made a rash (and black) joke about Hitler believing in 'giving every man his due'; and, a few years before, Sir Herbert Read, who had come over to open an exhibition of the White Stag Group, of which Ralph was a member, had to leave the house in a hurry because of some remark he was understood to have made about the later work of Marc Chagall being 'schmalz'.

Anti-semitism was practically a capital charge, and most people, grasping the dangers, took great pains to avoid any reference to the subject whatever. Yet this was difficult to do, for whether because his then wife, Nancy, was part

Jewish, or because he had spent part of his young manhood in Germany just before Hitler came to power, Ralph refused to let the matter alone. This would not have mattered so much except that any reference, even enthusiastic condemnation of racism of any sort, carried its dangers. Ralph could and would rant about anti-semitism to his heart's content. The guests dared not risk a comment of any description, for fear of misconstruction or misinterpretation. Thus a sort of final solution was arrived at by everybody but the host: as far as they were concerned the Jewish race had ceased to exist.

Many of his traumas were related, however obscurely, to the subject of money; and it, in general, was one best forgotten also. He was, or had been, a comparatively rich man; but he was patriarchal by nature; and more than one household was now dependent on him. He was therefore 'going into capital', a process which seems guaranteed to produce typhoons and earthquakes in the mentality of those engaged in it. Worse still, he had expectations. These hinged on the deaths of two very old and rich uncles who lived on opposite sides of Dublin bay: one in Howth and one in Killiney. The old uncle in Howth was free to leave him the money or not as he chose; the one in Killiney would have to do so, since it was entailed to Ralph, and it was only a question of waiting on, and if possible hastening, his death.

The two ends of the bay became therefore opposite poles in his psychology. The old uncle in Howth had to be visited regularly, cosseted and charmed. Little presents would be brought, family news exchanged, anecdotes of the far away and long ago dutifully listened to, the *persona* of the affectionate nephew adopted for the occasion. All this would of course be followed by a terrible revulsion of feeling; and, as like as not, Ralph would then get into his motor-car, drive all the way round the bay, and take it out on the other uncle, even going so far as to hurl stones and articles of garden furniture through his windows. The two uncles seemed to symbolise the Jekyll and Hyde duality in his nature and the mere thought of them to elicit startling transformations.

In order to stem the famous inroads into capital, he had gone into business of a sort. This was the selling of flower bulbs. To further it he issued an annual catalogue which was a masterpiece of description and prevarication. The charms and beauties of each flower, guaranteed to be actually 'growing wild somewhere', were described at length and at leisure in highly individual and persuasive prose. The conditions in which it grew best were stated. What was not quite clear was whether Ralph had ever succeeded in inducing it to grow at all. The bulbs he sold were imported from Holland. They arrived in large boxes, packed in a substance which looked like fragmented mica. The manual part of the business consisted in repacking these bulbs and sufficient of the substance to keep them going in smaller boxes, labelling these and posting them off to individual customers.

Outside in the garden large numbers of the flowers listed had once been planted and some of them, I believe, did really and truly grow there, though nobody ever seemed to go near them. I suppose, being wild flowers, the theory was that they could look after themselves. Occasionally enthusiasts who had received the catalogue would arrive and demand to be shown some rare Himalayan or Andean species, born evidently to blush unseen, or at least not available for inspection at that particular moment and time of year. During these visits Ralph was usually, to begin with, the very soul of courtesy, a fact which made the transition the more startling to the visitors when instead of an erudite, affable and charming Anglo-Irish country gentleman they found they had a snarling and raging maniac on their hands, who as like as not pursued them back to their motor-car with maledictions and animadversions on their general ignorance and presumption.

The unpacking and repacking of the bulbs involved quite an amount of labour and it was to help with this, at some stage when the wild flower business was apparently booming, that I was delicately recruited. At the same time the landlord from the Catacombs was brought out to do the cooking, all other hands being engaged with the boxes. It was a happy enough time, the more so since I was for some reason immune from the attacks that made most other people barricade their doors at night, or sit with an uneasy eye on the turf-basket and the coal scuttle, two favourite weapons of our host's. When not, however, engaged in upending the contents of the former over somebody's head, or wedging the latter firmly down over somebody's startled brows, Ralph was the soul of charm, a mine of curious information and a fount of anecdote. He had lived the life of his time as it had been lived by so many other intellectuals of his class, proceeding from a hated English public school to the enviable Mediterranean rock-pool, spending the immediate pre-Nazi period in Berlin and the uneasy peace of the Riveria. Like others of his ilk he had watched the death-throes of his world and been driven by the war to return to his homeland, the difference in his case being that the homeland was neutral Ireland, not embattled and rationed Britain. He possessed the usual Anglo-Irish ambiguity, hating the English for their dullness and hypocrisy, yet not feeling at home among the Catholic Irish either. He had been married in Berlin in 1933, one of the guests being a well-known Jewish novelist. When the wedding party returned from the registry office to the bride's apartment, somebody switched on the wireless. Hitler's voice could be heard: he had become Chancellor that morning and was ranting to the German people. The novelist put down his glass, went straight to his bank and from there to the railway station, never to return to Germany again. Ralph's Berlin was that of Christopher Isherwood; his Mediterranean a mixture of Connolly and Lawrence; for the untravelled, like myself, his talk was fascinating.

And in spite of the dangers to life and limb there was a constant stream of visitors to the house, for, outbreaks of violence apart, Ralph was exceedingly hospitable. It was an old haunt of Brendan's and it was associated in his mind with the idea of getting away from it all and actually doing some writing. This was an ambition not likely to be realised, for the drink flowed fast and furious, day and night; but nonetheless these visits to the country brought out the literary side of him and there he would talk perhaps more seriously about his ambitions than elsewhere.

Like all young writers worth their salt he was boundlessly ambitious, though he had little to show for it, and suffered,

21

like us all, from the apparently unending wastage of days. He suffered too, and perhaps more acutely than most, from the usual uncertainties about forms of expression. Though he wrote a few short stories he was never really an aspirant novelist. The elaborately developed, situation novel, with classified, ambition-motivated characters in a developing societal relationship, does not in any case suit the native genius, nurtured as it has been in anarchy, or in classless, largely propertyless, sloth, cheer and despair; and Brendan was more anarchic than most, and even less disciplined. He was also an anecdotalist, with countless characters at his command so far as their surface characteristics and modes of speech were concerned, but he had in those days no vision of a form that might contain his stories, his imitations, his parodies and the anarchic glee and comic life-apprehension that lay behind them. He might have found something of what he was looking for in Irish writers as different as Carleton, Lever and Somerville and Ross, but I do not think he had read these; and meantime he picked up *Pride and Prejudice* and looked into it with a sort of comic rage and dismay.

The Irish poems are melodic, and, so far as the expression of rather vague, diffused feeling can be, sincere, but they did not contain very much of the real man, and, though every young poet knows this gap and the feeling of despair that accrues from it–did not Yeats lament in his old age that we can only bring a very small part of the total personality to birth in poems?–Brendan, who had a very keen sense of himself as personality, who imagined, perhaps wrongly, that it was as a comic character, a creation of his own, that he shone or not at all, felt it more keenly than most.

Oddly enough, it was not until later that he really thought about the play as a kind of possible hold-all for his talents; though he asked me one day as we walked through the bare winter woods whether I thought 'all that business about stage-craft, getting people on and off and all that stuff' mattered and, if so, how would one go about learning it. I told him I thought it was mostly a mystique invented by professional playwrights and theatre folk to give themselves something to be exclusive about, and he seemed satisfied.

When he did write plays he got some part of the way towards what would have suited his genius—a sort of tragi-comic music hall with much of life's inconsequentiality and a lot of chat and song. But there were other factors operative by then, and not all of them were a help to him.

3

WHEN I came back from Roundwood, it was to find that life in the Catacombs had changed, and for the worse. In the landlord's absence one of his tenants had taken over the passages, sculleries, broom-cellars and all those tenements, demesnes and habiliments adjoining. Though of a different social order and racial stock, he was, like Ralph Cusack, of a patriarchal nature, and he had installed friends as well as family. He believed, as the native race always has, in sub-division, so the most you could get to yourself was a corner. Besides, the friends had been introduced and encouraged to stay in order to cow the landlord so the more there were of them, he thought, the merrier. Apart from McDaid's hangers-on, the news of an almost free kip had spread to old comrades down the country and many had come up to Dublin to disport themselves. They came from Erris, Clare and Kerry, Connemara and the isles; the nearest some of them had ever previously been to Dublin was during intern-ment or in prison; they were of a much less sophisticated nature than the old denizens of the place; they brought in outsiders nightly and their idea of entertainment was to fight, with fists, bottles and boots, endlessly, monotonously and, what was worse, predictably.

It was during this period that the Catacombs began to acquire a hitherto undeserved reputation for violence and other things; cheerful enough though it was sometimes, the place no longer suited the contemplative disposition. It was time to move on. A friend of mine, also an ex-internee, who was caretaker of a house in Waterloo Road, offered me the use of a sort of shed or concrete hutment at the bottom of the garden. It was agreed that Peter Walsh, formerly Officer

Commanding Dartmoor, and I, should share it, paying five shillings a week each towards a total of ten. Actually Peter was more or less ensconced in neo-domestic circumstances at the time, so he was seldom there. I had, however, plenty of guests of the homeless variety. Chief among these was Brendan.

'The Gurriers'—as Peter soon christened my new abode— had no furniture except a small table, a sort of folding chair and, for some reason, a three-tiered iron bed. This peculiar bunkment had mattresses, but no covering. In the course of time, however, I acquired various rugs, small carpets, discarded window curtains and other oddments, sufficient to give myself and a guest or two something to huddle under. One had to remain clothed of course. Apart from the cold in the winter time, one needed something between the skin and the texture of a carpet or floor-mat.

In the summer time it was pleasant enough. There were trees outside and bird-song, and though in those days I was not much of a one for the morning choirings, it was nice enough to lie in the top bunk with the sun streaming through the big window, particularly if you had a few bob and cheerful companionship.

Brendan was at his best and most philosophical in the mornings, waking up like the birds with jokes and generalisations apparently matured in sleep. In 'The Gurriers' lay a solitary review copy: indeed, not to put too fine a tooth on it, a solitary book. This was a reissue of Frank Swinnerton's *The Georgian Literary Scene*. I had read it in adolescence and been entranced by what I thought was a picture of the real world of letters, the magic circle into which one sought to enter. For old time's sake I had snaffled the book in the offices of a literary magazine, brought it back to my humble abode and retained it. It was meat and drink to Brendan.

Every morning, as we lay under our assorted coverings, he would regale me with extracts describing the country homes, the habits of composition, the attitudes and the mannerisms of the writers, many of them minor, of the first thirty years of the century. This was the world of letters. Here were our sorry selves. Passages describing visits to John Drinkwater or Ralph Hodgson in their rural retreats, an encounter with Hilaire Belloc or a conversation with Arnold Bennett would become a theme of fantasy. He would affect a manner of conversation which had belonged to some notability of the nineteen-twenties and speak about his person and creative problems as if he were Norman Douglas. A description of the droop in the eyelids of some hard-working novelist, which, according to Swinnerton, was the result of sitting over the typewriter all day while the smoke curled upwards from the cigarette between his lips, especially appealed to him; and in McDaid's Brendan would adopt the drooping eyelids and demand to be told what caused them. After all had guessed he would declare that it came from sitting over the typewriter all day while the smoke curled upwards etc.

One chapter of Swinnerton's book concerned a school of First World War poets, Robert Nichols and others, who wrote short, futurist-imagist poems which tried to recapture the realities of trench life by reproducing its sounds. When we sallied forth into the streets Brendan would stop somebody, perhaps some civil servant or other of our acquaintance, and ask if he would like to hear a new poem. The fellow, who perhaps had a literary reputation to keep up, would acquiesce, at least after a fashion. Brendan would then raise his head, gaze into the middle distance and pause—all of which in the other party's judgment was the proper procedure before reciting—and then proceed to emit a series of sounds meant to represent anything from love-making to the pulling of a pint. There would follow another pause while the audience, imagining that some complicated throat-clearing ceremony was being gone through, waited in vain. Then he would be asked what he thought and, if necessary, the theory of the thing explained to him. 'Oh come on now, Brendan, you can do better than that', was once the patient enough reply.

One Sunday morning we left 'The Gurriers' together and walked down Waterloo Road towards Mooneys. It was a fine sunny afternoon—we would have called it morning—but Sunday was the most miserable day of the week. The opening hours being half-past-one to three and five to seven, the only hours the Archbishop would allow because they were the only hours of the day when a Catholic service of some kind was not proceeding somewhere in the city of Dublin. For this reason one's opportunities on a Sunday were seriously limited. There was, as Brendan used to say, 'no place to sit and beg'.

We had only a few shillings and it was a serious matter whether to buy a Sunday newspaper or not. Eventually we decided to buy a *Sunday Times* and as we sat over two pints and the divided paper we discovered that George Orwell was dead. 'Listen to this, Brendan', I said, and I read him the closing passage of Cyril Connolly's famous obituary: 'But the gardens of the west are closed, and there is no place now for the writer to wander . . .' A look of intense fury came over Brendan's face. 'Arrah sweet and holy Jasus, would you mind telling me what fucking gardens of the west did you and I ever wander in?' he asked.

Yet in fact that summer we did go for a sort of a walk in the gardens of the west together, even if it wasn't of the idyllic kind Connolly had in mind. One day, as we lay on our bunks in 'The Gurriers', Brendan asked me if I would like to come to Paris. He had published a very short story in *Envoy* and George Morrison, later to be the creator of the well-known newsreel *collage* 'Mise Éire', had offered him forty pounds for the right to make a small film of it. Forty pounds, he admitted, wasn't a whole lot for a protracted stay for the two of us, but he had a scheme in mind which had immense possibilities. If we played our cards right we might get to spend a year or two on the Continent. Pressed to explain, he tittered to himself in a way he had and said that we were going 'to snatch the Pope's ring'. Then he said darkly that what he had in mind was political. Finally that he would unfold his plan when we got to Paris. It was the sort of thing that if anybody in Dublin got to hear of it we were 'fucked from a height'. I might as well come along to Paris anyway and make up my mind about the rest when we got there.

Well, I had a reason of my own for wanting to get to Paris, apart from the very good one that I had never been there; I was always game for a jaunt in good company; and in those days I was always glad to get out of Ireland. I agreed. Time, like Brendan, was to be merciful in its disclosures.

27

A couple of nights later we got seats on an Aer Lingus plane to London. Brendan was equipped with a fairly sizeable cardboard suitcase and a sort of duffle bag. I wondered at the size of the luggage, as, later that night, I was to wonder at the number of dirty shirts, legs of pyjamas, disreputable underwear and odd socks he had brought, and at the inclusion in the suitcase of the remains of a suit which was certainly no better than the one he had on. Even if we were planning on a two-year stay, I thought, we should be able to pick up things as we went along. I did not know that in the place he had in mind there was supposed to be a shortage of wearing apparel as well as everything else.

Besides the luggage he had the forty pounds, our tickets to London having been paid for by Ralph Cusack. I had a small zip bag with a shirt or two and four or five pounds besides. Brendan therefore had nearly all the money; and he had also all, or nearly all, the French, which was little enough.

We were slightly drunk getting on the plane and as soon as it was off the ground he applied the Voltairean test to God's existence, rising in his seat, clenching his small fists, glaring at the roof and challenging the deity to prove his power by causing the machine to crash. It was not logical that the test should be more conclusive when applied in the more perilous circumstance of being airborne in a man-made contraption than it would if we had been like Voltaire in the middle of a field, but you never know. Fortunately he did not seem to be overheard either by the deity or by the two elderly priests behind us for whose benefit the performance was put on.

In London we stayed the night with an Irish doctor of my acquaintance, sleeping what sleep we slept on the floor of his Swiss Cottage flat, and in the morning we got the wrong bus for Victoria. We stood on an island in the middle of the Strand, I remember, unable to get across, while the traffic roared past, Brendan hurling curses at the double-deckers with raised fists, reviling the English and their ways, engaged in a titanic contest of wills with all the might of the Empire's capital. Finally we got a taxi, in which I, that was supposed to have lived there, was attacked for my inadequate knowledge of London. It was the first time that the-man-of-action-thwarted-by-inadequate-lieutenant streak in him showed up; but it was not to be the last, and in France he had the advantage that he spoke, or fancied he spoke, the French, had been there before and had the money.

At Newhaven we ran into what looked like trouble. Brendan was a deportee from England, released from Borstal originally only on condition that he did not return to its shores. Fairly stiff penalties would attend on the discovery that he had done so; and though it was unlikely that the authorities were at that time still on the *qui vive* for him or anyone else in his category there was a good deal about us to attract attention. Anyway, we had no sooner put our tawdry baggage down on the counter for examination by the ordinary customs man than another official in plain clothes came over, said something to him, and asked politely if he could have a word with us. We went a little way up the counter with him and he examined our passports closely. Then he asked us to turn out the contents of our pockets. Unfortunately Brendan carried a painter's trade-union card which was made out in another name: he was not a proper, dues-paid member of the union in his own right. The official, who had not seemed to attach any importance to the name Behan, remarked on the discrepancy in names between card and passport. Behan proffered an involved, hurried but skilfully contrived explanation to the effect that he was a stepson and that in Ireland a stepson commonly used his mother's original name for certain purposes and his father's for certain others. This was received with the sort of silent interest only authority can assume.

Then it was my turn. Among my bits and pieces happened to be a letter from David Marcus, then editor of *Irish Writing*, about the proofs of some poems he had accepted. Our friend's eyes positively lit up.

'You are a poet, Mr Cronin?' he asked.

I assented to the description in some stumbling form or other. He gazed upon us both for a moment with smiling, considering lips, then handed back what he held and motioned us graciously to proceed.

It was a moment of great relief and we were pleased also to see that the boat flew the French flag, but as we boarded

29

it Brendan turned and complained. 'You might have told the limey bastard your disreputable friend was a poet too', he said.

We crossed Paris in sunlight, on the back of a bus, from the Gare du Nord to the Luxembourg, a route that took us round the Place de la Concorde and past the Tuileries. Nobody could ever forget such a first sight of the city, but this isn't that kind of travel book, nor, either, an autobiography, so suffice it to say here that Brendan enjoyed my enjoyment to the full. He had, after all, a proprietary interest in the place.

It was traditional among such McDaideans as ever got to Paris (which in accordance with a Joycean, pro-European, anti-British bias was a thing to do) to stay at the Hotel du Grand Balcon, in the street of the same name, by the Danton statue, in the heart of the Latin Quarter. In those days cheap left-bank hotels really were cheap and they always, even in summer, had room. The left bank itself was still, to some extent, enjoying its post-war, G.I. Bill, literary efflorescence. *Points* and *Merlin* were, I think, to come later, as was George's bookshop, the first beats and juke-boxes in the bars. Styron, Baldwin and Mailer were to establish a new Paris tradition of a sort, but in those days newcomers were for the most part still sustained by the old one. Such Americans as we drank with still wore army shirts and trousers and were re-living an ancient departure, sitting in the Dome or the Coupole, the soft glow of the late-night neon a cocoon for dreams of Hem and Scott, Harry Crosby or Henry Miller. Drinking the last *fine* in the Select at three o'clock in the morning while the chairs were piled up on the tables and the lights went out up the street, adjourning to Les Halles for the onion soup which was still within the means of the poorest, going on to somebody's place to continue the argument or pursue the conquest, many Americans, and others too, knew that Paris was what it was all about.

We did not, I am afraid, succeed in establishing ourselves sexually or socially in any snug little circle of beauty and booze. We snatched at what offered of course, but for a man who had been there before Brendan seemed pretty short of acquaintance. Perhaps there really wasn't any bohemia of our sort to enter. Most of the people we did meet were Americans. They lived in hotel rooms like ourselves and they were all meditating great books. Some of them were to write best-sellers but the manifestations of the new, post-Hem and Scott Paris were not of great interest. I remember thinking one night when we were ejected from a folk-song cellar somewhere round the Place St. Germain that the audience did not compose, as they would say now-adays, our scene. We were not to know it then, but we were witnessing the birth of the new bohemia, which would not even pay lip-service to any form of art other than the most rudimentary kinds of music.

Meanwhile, of course, there was Brendan's grand design to be meditated. He unfolded it on the first day and it took my breath away. Like most grand designs it was bold and cunning, simple and tortuous all at once. In case I did not know, we were in the middle of the Marian Holy Year. The Faithful were exhorted to make pilgrimages to Rome while the year lasted and encouraged by great remittances of the time they would have to spend in Purgatory to do so. We too would head out for the Holy City, begging for food and shelter like mediaeval palmers. The decent pious people of France and their priests would fall over themselves to provide two devout Irish pilgrims with bed and board. There would be free lodging and hot scoff at every turn of the road. We would have a few weeks' luxury in the French countryside, perhaps a little tour in Italy itself, but that was not all he had in mind. We would traverse Northern Italy, go as far eastward as seemed plausible, and then make a dash for Czechoslovakia. We would cross the Czech frontier, declare ourselves to be refugees from Western Capitalism and abandon ourselves to the mercy of events. We were not, it was true, as eminent as we might be, but we were published writers; we would be among the first such defectors from the West; and surely to God they would find some use for us, in their radio stations or whatever they had.

My notions of geography were a little clearer than Brendan's and I could see he was skimping the last stages. Besides, my ideological feelings were not as orthodox, or indeed as strong. I did not like the sound of the Czechs. And would not they be rather puzzled by the idea of refugees from the West, where after all there was supposed to be freedom of speech? To this last Brendan replied that at least we would have had a jaunt. Somebody would have to repatriate us and probably in a blaze of glory. He was admittedly a little dubious about the reaction of the Czech authorities; indeed he was dubious about the Czechs in general, describing them in the next breath as 'Russians with Manchester accents', but they would hardly be likely to mistake us for spies.

At length we agreed to postpone the Czech side of the journey for further consideration and to make use of the Holy Year along the lines suggested. We would head out, try to get to Rome, and see what, in the contemporary phrase, 'gave' there. It might be that monasteries and like institutions in the Holy City itself would put pilgrims up for nothing, and that by ringing the changes on the possibilities we could get a summer out of it. Certainly, as pilgrims, we ought to be able to make it; we would see a bit of historic-and-whatever-else France and Italy; and if we had to be repatriated in the end by the Irish Embassy we would at least have got value for their money. What, in any case, else could we do? We were down to our last few pounds, and Paris, in spite of its traditions of literary and artistic poverty, was not proving a great source of possibilities.

And I had another reason for getting out. I had come in hope, and the hope had vanished. I was slightly in love with an American girl who lived in Paris but had spent a while in Dublin that summer; and I had had her address and lost it. She lived, I knew, somewhere in one of the narrow streets on the islands and I must have searched them all, asking wherever I could. On the third day I found the place. The proprietress said she had moved, leaving no forwarding address but the American Express. I went there daily, left notes and waited. There were other American girls to look at, the iced water to drink. I was fond of American girls at the time: even the barbarous accents of the middle-west did not dismay me. Quite the contrary. The girls that summer wore either white shorts with turned-up edges, or sleeveless, severe linen dresses; they had long, sun-tanned arms and legs; and there were many of them. But mine never came. I walked vaguely round the Left Bank and sat down in cafés to enquire about her from likely-looking compatriots. In the end I found the small hotel she had moved to, but she was gone home. *'Mariée.'* I had thought she might be, since she spoke of the possibility. Paris under the blazing August sky was slightly darkened, slightly enhanced by the circumstance.

Meanwhile Brendan conceived the extraordinary notion that I had found her; that I was holding out on him; and that during my absences I was in receipt of meals, favours, consolations, money even, denied to him; when in fact all I was doing was walking round like an idiot.

It was time to go. South or east, Mother Church or Communist Party, it was all one to me. *'Nous nous marchons'* I said one day in the Deux Magots under the impression that it meant 'we must march' and that a general had said it. It became our slogan and Brendan used it for years afterwards to indicate that it was time to leave one bar for another.

We took the Metro to Orly and walked out a bit. A large van stopped and after some negotiation the driver, who wanted money, seemed unimpressed by the fact that we were pilgrims and said he was going to Marseilles, lowered the back and indicated a small space already occupied by a thirsty and hungry looking Alsatian. No dog-lovers, we refused. Then the driver of a battered vegetable lorry picked us up and took us through the verdant forest of Fontainebleau and all the way to Sens. We made it eventually through the cooling twilight to Auxerre, where we slept beneath a wall on a steep grass bank sloping down to the river, the Cathedral above us under the stars, the big *camions* roaring through the night. We had covered the best part of a hundred miles and felt we were in the provinces. I said Belloc's poem 'When Peter Wanderwide was thrown by death itself beyond Auxerre' as a sort of night prayer for the pilgrims.

In fact the pilgrimage proper only began the following day and it was almost immediately obvious that it was not going to live up to expectations. The response of the French to the statement that we were *'deux Irlandaises en perinage a Rome'*, which was the way Brendan put it, was at best indifferent. They did not show the same interest or enthusiasm, he remarked bitterly, 'as our own people would have done if any of them were passing through Holy Ireland on a pilgrimage to the North Pole'; in fact, not to put too fine a tooth upon it, 'the fuckers wouldn't give you the steam off their piss.' However, lifts could be got, though not always in the required direction, and not because we were pilgrims; and on the night after Auxerre we found a parish priest who allowed us to sleep on wooden forms put together in some sort of a schoolhouse. He was the first of a line of more or less sympathetic clerics. 'The priests are with the people still,' as Brendan put it, echoing an old Irish patriotic song.

This was in Autun, the city where Talleyrand was bishop before he went off to survive. We didn't know this of course, though in fact we behaved like orthodox tourists here for once and climbed a terribly steep hill on a terribly hot day to visit the Cathedral, which was cool at least, whether twelfth century, as I said, or thirteenth, as Brendan, who had the French, insisted. We were remarkably ignorant of most things, indeed a more unprepared, unlearned, and therefore largely blind pair of travellers it would have been hard to find. So far from having a guidebook to give us any historical or other information about places on the way, we hadn't even a map, and were in Autun only by accident. Our ignorance did not prevent us from arguing, however, in the heat or in the rain.

A pattern of days established itself. We worked south, as far as we could, eating bread, tomatoes, cheese and sausage, drinking much wine and a little milk. At evening we would seek out a curé wherever we happened to be and Brendan would say his piece about 'deux Irlandaises' etc. If this worked, which be it said again for the reverend gentlemen it very often did, we got put up on floors in draughty parish halls, in outhouses; even, as with some truly delightful worker priests in Lyons, in a bed for two nights. If it didn't, we stayed either in the cheapest auberge we could find or slept out, as once on some municipal benches opposite a bakery which opened while it was still dark and perfumed the air all about with the most exquisite scent of fresh bread.

Of course we had neither tents nor sleeping bags, cooking

utensils, water bottles or stoves. We were dressed as we had been in Dublin and the baggage we carried contained nothing that was of the remotest use to men camping out. Compared to the professional hitchhikers of to-day, even to such youth-hostellers as we encountered then, we were as two dudes in the American west.

Still, we edged on, erratically and not too hurriedly, through little towns which smelled at dusk of soup and sewage, through Chalons-sur-Saone, where it rained ('a dirty kip, like a little bit of old Brum'), Mâcon, Villefranche, where they were firing off guns ('to keep the rain away from the grapes'), Lyons, where in a café with the worker priests Brendan took to the Ricard ('the nearest thing to absinthe you can get'), knocking it back like so many *poètes maudits* before him had knocked back the real stuff. He explained to them aspects of his political philosophy: 'Communism will not come terrible like an army with banners, but like a Corporation dustman carting off the rubbish of the ages.' In Grenoble he insisted on going up in a cable car to see what he said was Mont Blanc in the distance. I had already had my first glimpse of the Alps from on top of an uncertain balanced heap of coal in the back of a speeding lorry. They were the largest mountains I had ever then seen and lightning was playing along their mass. To make things more terrifying, we were in a blinding rainstorm, which increased the difficulty of hanging on to the coal, as well as the discomfort of it, until the driver stopped and insisted that there was room in front for all three of us and the bags, which when he got in there originally Brendan had declared loudly there was not.

In Grenoble we found a café full of drunks, men and women who composed some sort of family party and took us home with them to sing 'Chevaliers de la Table Ronde' and other songs familiar in the Catacombs ('It's well known in Holy Ireland that you would never see a Frenchman drunk'). At Briançon we were reluctantly admitted into a youth hostel ('My father was a founder of the youth movement in Ireland—he was too, ye sniggering Judas, leastways he was in the Fianna'). And after Briançon, within a few miles of the long-awaited Italian frontier, we quarrelled.

It was a silly business, about one of the bags which had been left behind in a café; but it was incredibly hot; we had walked a long way out of town to begin with and then had to walk back for the bag; and we were both hung over. Anyway there was some shouted recrimination and insult. Brendan then for the first time divided up the money, which amounted to very little, and headed back for town. I stood alone by the side of the road for a while and then I went after him. I searched the empty cafés in the noonday heat, but I had left it too late. I decided out of some stubborn principle, and because there seemed little else to do, to go on into Italy.

This is not my story. If it were I would describe the effect a first introduction to that great and gracious land has on the traveller. I crossed the Col di Tenda in the car of an Italian who was going home and came down on the iridescent plains of Piedmont and Lombardy as the weary, exiled Irish anchorites must have come down in the eighth century. Everyone smiled; you waved and everyone waved back; everyone was excited; it was not like France. I tried the *perinage à Roma* and it worked, even with a communist lorry driver who insisted on buying the wine. Then out of principle I gave it up, except of course with people of a religious disposition. I stayed for two days at a monastery near Carmagnola—in which town there was a horse fair— and I got as far as Milan. I travelled with all sorts of people and I listened with understanding to that language which everybody can understand. I was attacked by a savage dog in a field; I was reprimanded by the police for sleeping on the plinth of a war memorial in Vigevano; but everything in Italy was in those days magical: ox-carts, mules, heavy hot-scented nights, Maseratis, Communism, the Cathedral in Milan.

And there I turned back. The money was almost gone and it looked a long way to Rome on the map. *Perinage* or no *perinage,* in Paris I had some sort of acquaintance. I went down through Genoa and Savona and so along the French Riviera to Aix-en-Provence, where I slept under a Roman arch beside the amphitheatre. Next morning I was picked up by a French couple who gave me wine and bread and paté by the roadside and took me all the way to Paris. They

Brendan Behan.

were young; they spoke English; they were obviously very much in love; and out of the goodness of their lovers' hearts they asked me what part of Paris I wanted to be dropped in. It was well after two o'clock in the morning when we arrived; I had no money at all now and no place to go; but I said the Left Bank and they took me there, dropping me at the corner of Montparnasse and the Boulevard St. Michel.

The Dome and the Select, the gardens of the west, were closing, the waiters piling up the chairs, and needless to say there was nobody I knew in either. It was raining and in front of me stretched the wide expanse of the Boul' Mich' with only the lights of Duponts still shining. Since I had to go some place I started to walk down towards the Boulevard St. Germain. I had passed Duponts when I heard my name called in unmistakable hoarse, Dublin tones. It was Brendan. He had been sitting all alone in the café, the last customer, and seen me, to his amazement, pass by in the rain. It was a truly extraordinary coincidence, and whatever recriminations there might have been in other circumstances we both, I think, felt only an immense relief. Apart from anything else, there is, after all, safety in numbers. Though he was almost penniless too, having slept out the night before, he had the price of a drink, and over it, he told me his story.

After he left me, he said, he had made his way without much difficulty back as far as Lyons. There he got to drinking the Ricard again. When he was penniless, or nearly so, he came across a Foreign Legion barracks which had a recruiting office and he promptly joined up. He was a member of the Legion for one night. P. C. Wren, it appeared, did not know what he was talking about. If you went to them in the morning 'in a dacent and civil manner', they speeded you on your way without even asking for the return of the bounty money. Whether this is true or not I do not know. Probably what happened was that the Foreign Legion found it had met its match. Some aspect of the protean Brendan had disquieted it, perhaps even characteristic verbal advances to a young comrade.

In any case, as time went by he became increasingly proud of having been a member of the corps, and the time spent under the tricolour hearing the bugles blow was suitably lengthened. Three years later I was sitting in a pub in London with the poet W. R. Rodgers. He began to reprove me, as he frequently did, for my then way of life. Why wouldn't I be adventurous, he said, and go away and join the Foreign Legion for a while, like Brendan Behan? The main agony, in most company, is caused by misconceptions which it is impossible to set right without appearing strident.

Anyway, after his term of service with the colours he had made his way back to Paris where he had been for a while, found a kip, borrowed some money and spent it. Then he went to the Embassy, got his repatriation money, and spent that too. Now he had nowhere to go.

We spent the remainder of that night on the embankment. In the morning I had a terrible toothache. Brendan was most solicitous, hunting up aspirins and buying me brandy with the last few francs. Then he suggested that I should go to the Embassy and get my repatriation money too. Meanwhile we decided that we would move into the Hotel d'Alsace down the street from the Grand Balcon. It had a reputation for being liberal with the credit and it must have been a long standing one, for it was here that our colleague and compatriot Oscar Wilde had died a little over half a century before. He was far behind with the rent and had replied to the landlord, when told he must either pay or go: 'Certainly, either I or the wallpaper must go.' It was from his darkened room there too that he had sent Robbie Ross out for a last bottle of champagne, saying, 'I fear, Robbie, I am dying as I have lived—beyond my means.' The thought of Oscar's difficulties was somehow comforting, though it seemed to me that we were now somewhat lower down in the circumstantial scale than he had ever got. Before we left Paris for the first time we had made a pilgrimage to his grave in Père Lachaise and asked his protection on our knees by the graveside. Brendan later wrote a poem in Gaelic, perhaps the best of all his poems, which takes the inscription on the wall of the Hotel d'Alsace for its epigraph: *Oscar Wilde, Poète et Dramaturge, né à Dublin le 15 Octobre, 1856, est mort dans cette maison le 30 Novembre, 1900.*

The place did not appear to have changed much since 1900; they let us in for the time being; and I went to the

Embassy. Instructed in the drill by Brendan, who waited on a bench in the boulevard, I was civilly enough received, given some Afton Major cigarettes—a brand which was to crop up again in our subsequent adventures—and told to come back in the afternoon. We walked round the area to pass the time and when I went back I was given ten pounds, or enough to get us both back to Ireland if we hitched and crossed the two seas by boat, supposing Brendan was willing to risk the passage through England. We discussed this and decided that the risk was minimal. Accordingly it was agreed to leave the next day.

We went back to the hotel, paid the bill up to the following morning and then went out to have the famous Alsatian sausages and wine by the tumbler at Le Petit Source which were everybody's main source of sustenance. We were in fine fettle, having money, a night in clean sheets and a journey over land and sea to look forward to.

Naturally we went on drinking. Then something odd began to happen. We went into a succession of small cafés round the river side of St. Germain. In each one Brendan insisted on buying drinks for the workmen at the zinc, talking his French, singing his songs and making his jokes. My remonstrations were met with anger and impatience, so I gave them up. Finally we wound up in a small place with a two-o'clock licence where there were about six men at the counter, one of whom unfortunately had a fiddle. Brendan ordered glasses all round and then began to buy wine by the bottle. To show both knowledge and generosity he asked for a particular *appellation controllée* wine of which they seemed to have a lot, and which certainly cost a lot comparatively. At two o'clock the proprietor put up the shutters and closed the door. The man with the fiddle played; everybody sang; and bottles began to appear with the speed of light.

I was now slightly drunk, miserable and angry, but every time I made a protest Brendan would ignore it and immediately order another bottle. I suppose I could have called a halt and walked out into the night with what money was left, but I knew there would be a scene and in the midst of all the jollification and bad French I was weak enough not to want to appear angry or upset or mean. Once when I tried to pay the remainder of the bill and be done with it Brendan spoke volubly to the proprietor who, instead of producing the bill brought out two more bottles. Yet he was not enjoying himself; that I could see. Behind all the pseudo-generosity, the songs and toasts and exchanges of national good will, there was something frantic. It began to dawn on me that it was also something destructive, and this was a new side of him. He wanted to get rid of the money and get back into what was certainly going to be the gutter.

I have always been helpless before others' hysteria–a weapon of which, in later days, Brendan was to make full use–and after a while I gave up; even trying to enjoy myself as he sang all his old Catacombs songs, 'Slievenamon', 'Preab San Ól', 'The Mountain Dew', as well as his considerable repertoire of French ones; the fiddler fiddled; and the others indulged him to the top of his bent. About half past three or so I knew our ruin was well accomplished; and when, sometime after four, the proceedings broke up, this proved to be, alas, the case. We had about two thousand francs left. Journeys by sea were out, whatever about journeys by land.

Next morning there was no repentance, but, as I presume would be the case after suicide, there was no satisfaction either. I had the grace to refrain from saying what I felt, but it was agreed that our journey would have to be, to say the least, postponed until further supplies were got. We felt so bad that it was agreed we should stay in the hotel one more night. Then the *boue* for which there had been so much *nostalgie* the night before would, as far as I could see, have been achieved.

Sometime during the course of the day, however, Brendan came up with another of his startling original ideas, almost comparable to the pilgrimage, or the political sanctuary, or the foreign legion. We would hitchhike to Rouen, from which port the boats owned by the Irish shipping company sailed regularly. On one of these we would stow away. When the ship was irrevocably at sea we would reveal ourselves, appeal to the racial compassion of all concerned and having successfully elicited it, arrive in Ireland of the welcomes hale, fresh and hearty after a salubrious sea-voyage.

Once more I fell in with the plan of the master. Whatever the degradations attached to stowing away—and I fancied there would be more than Brendan in his enthusiasm bargained for—we had very little alternative. While we discussed the matter Brendan suggested that he might get money for the journey to Rouen from a lady writer with whom he had become acquainted during his first visit to Paris. Is it possible that it was Simone de Beauvoir, or is it only the imagination of retrospect that suggests that to me? Anyway, he went off to find her while I remained in a pre-ordained spot, drinking, I may say, as slowly as possible, but, as was only fair after the night before, drinking nonetheless. *Au bout de compte,* after the night before I felt I was justified. It took him hours to come back, and when he did he had bad news. The lady writer, Simone de Beauvoir or otherwise, was out of town, and would be until the day after to-morrow. We decided on an alternative. In Dublin our mutual friend Eddie Chapman, the famous secret agent, had told us that if we were badly stuck for money in Paris we could go to M'sieu somebody or other who ran the concession bar in the Georges Cinque hotel and use his name and his credit. M'sieu whoever it was would not refuse.

Perhaps Eddie had not foreseen that our general appearance would now be what it was; perhaps he had exaggerated M'sieu so-and-so's readiness to extend credit to his more *outré* friends.

Around nine o'clock we set off for the Georges Cinque, which is of course off the Champs Elysées, away over on the right bank and a considerable distance from where we were. We had to walk through the neon-lit evening scene to get there and it took us over an hour.

It was decided on the way that I should make the approach and when we got to the hotel I strode as boldly as I could into the lobby. I had the benefit of a few drinks. The lobbies of large hotels are confusing anyway and among the multiplicity of signs, mirrors, lounges and corridors in that regal establishment I could not immediately see where to go. A flunkey came over and addressed me in French. I replied in English that I wished to see M'sieu whatnot of the such and such bar. He looked at me as if I was something the cat of the house had unfortunately just brought in, but perhaps impressed sufficiently by the English, he told me, in English, to follow him. So far so good, but instead of leading me across the lobby to where we eventually wound up, he led me around behind the ornate pillars which flanked it, thus keeping me, as far as possible, out of sight of the legitimate customers.

Demoralised, I descended the staircase he indicated and found M'sieu whoever he was among his customers, bottles, trays, underlings, dim lights and reflecting surfaces. I will say he listened. He listened in English and in silence, that silence which barmen as well as policemen know how to assume. Then he asked me where M'sieu Eddie was at the moment. I replied foolishly that I did not know. The Eddie changed ominously to Chapman as he raised his French eyebrows and asked how it was that I did not know? I told him that M'sieu Eddie moved about a lot and he replied dryly that yes indeed he knew that, he did. Did I know when he would be next in Paris? If I had had a titter of wit I would of course have said next week. Instead I told him humbly that again I did not know. He replied curtly that what I asked was impossible. That was that. Before he could, I walked away.

Brendan took the news in good part, but of course I exaggerated slightly the persuasiveness and resource I had shown. We walked back down the long length of the Champs Elysées, past the cheerful concourses at the café tables, the beautiful girls being handed from taxis, the illuminated jewellery in the shop windows. We had practically no money and no beds to go to, but it was a warm, silky summer night and somehow we got into good humour along the way. When we reached the Place de la Concorde we took a path that led across the centre through the grass and sat under the trees talking about literature. Around us in a wide circle went the dimmed headlights of the traffic; beyond them were the famous restaurants that fringe the Place; in front stretched the wide, neon-lit boulevard of the rich and restless.

The word 'sincerity' got into the talk: a fundamental matter, if an unlikely one in the surroundings. It seemed to bother Brendan and his bother seemed to arise out of more than the ordinary 'fiction' versus 'truth' conflict. He asked me a curious question: naïve but illuminating. If I were given the choice between being a great writer, poor and unrecognised, or being someone who was praised and fêted, but who knew himself that he was a failure, and even a fraud, which would I choose? With the summer night about us and the lights still on in Maxim's and the Tour d'Argent, I said I thought one would be better off being the first fellow. After a long pause he said quietly that he was not so sure.

In the days of his fame afterwards, the days of the edited ramblings and the rewriting geniuses of the London theatre, I often thought of that conversation. Was it in part the gap between his actual achievement and his ridiculous reputation that made him destroy himself? Money and fame are not necessarily bad things, yet Brendan paid the highest price for them and put them to appalling use. The devils of the fame-making apparatus and the Dublin Faustus they chose may have been made for each other, but as always Faustus got the worst of the bargain.

Well, I have said it was a warm night, and we decided like many other denizens of Paris that night that there was nothing for it but to sleep out. We agreed on the embankment under the arches of the Pont Neuf, a place which was roofed at least and sheltered to some extent from gaze. Usually when I slept out, which I had been doing fairly frequently in the last few weeks, I took off my shoes. I had a theory that the whole body kept warmer if the blood circulated freely through the extremities. It was then my practice to put my feet in the hood of the old duffle-coat I wore and to cover the rest of myself with the body of it and anything else to hand. So, as we put on Brendan's spare shirts and made bedding and pillows out of such other garments as we had between us, I blithely took off my shoes and put them down beside me. When we woke to the early morning noises of the city they were gone. During the night some poor poverty-stricken, perhaps shoeless, fellow-man must have crept fearfully and delicately up to us and nipped them.

Thus began three days of macabre misery. In the large suitcase Brendan had a spare pair of shoes, as he had had a spare pair of everything in order to be decently accoutred when we went to stay with Czechs. He fished them out now but a glance showed the truth. They were about size five. I take size nine, and they were narrow in proportion to their length, quite natty and pointed in fact. I could wedge my feet only a little way into them and my heels projected over the backs. I could, and did, partly flatten the backs, but I still couldn't ram my feet far enough forward for the shoes to lift when I lifted my feet. The best I could manage was a ridiculous sort of sliding or skating motion, pushing foot and shoe together forward along the ground. For the next three days that was how I locomoted.

And for the next three days it rained. We eked out the barest of existences by begging occasional small sums from our scanty and not very prosperous acquaintance. Into most of the more reputable cafés I was refused admission because of my general appearance and ridiculous shuffling gait. Brendan would go off for long periods in search of Madame de Beauvoir or some other chimera and I, whose mobility was limited, would wait in the rain on boulevard benches, in the American library or even in the Christian Science reading room. Each night we slept under the arch of the Pont Neuf. Miss de Beauvoir (if that is who it was) remained in the country. We had reached the nadir of our fortunes.

On the fourth day she returned. She even–if it was she–accompanied him to the Boulevard St. Germain, where I sat on my bench. He introduced me as an Irish poet. She said she preferred her poets to look like businessmen. Then she departed and Brendan disclosed that for whatever reason–his diffidences, concealments and poverties of spirit, or her parsimony–he had got only five thousand francs, or five pounds in English money.

Still, it was enough to implement the new grand design; and with the rain lifting and Paris, that lamp for lovers lit in the wood of the world, beginning to shine again, we took the road–or rather, to begin with at least, the Metro.

It was a pleasant journey. In a dump by the roadside at Orly we found a pair of former Wellingtons with the tops unevenly hacked off which fitted me after a fashion. I did not have to skate along the ground any longer. We reached

45

Rouen in two days, spending the night between in the scented warmth and luxury of a hay-barn, and had happy memories of Normandy and the Normans. Whoever said it about them, whatever Flaubert might insinuate, the inhabitants of those wide flat fields and owners of gigantic ploughhorses were not mean. They gave us strong cider and even buttermilk at farmhouse doors, and if we had a little Calvados in the cobbled streets of Les Andelys or Sotteville who shall blame us? We were, we happily thought, on the way home.

In Rouen it was raining again, but there, tied up by the broad river and a lesson for the eyes of the sceptic of the party to behold, was an Irish ship: let us call it the 'Irish Scrub'. Brendan was considerably elated and inclined to crow over any doubts I had expressed. There remained of course the minor problem of getting on board.

Opposite the ship was a sort of shed with a projecting roof running round it and here we sheltered for a few minutes while we debated the matter. Then two sailors came down the gangway and headed off up the quay towards the town. 'Dubb-el-in men', said Brendan, and was after them like a flash, leaving his two bags on the ground beside me.

He who hesitates is lost indeed, and in this case I hesitated too long, running a few uncertain steps after him as he caught up with the sailors and disappeared into the grey rain; calling out vainly as he walked with them gesturing; and returning then miserably to the bags. I was in for a wait, but I didn't know how long it was going to be.

A half-hour passed by a clock I could hear somewhere; then another and another. I took short walks in the direction in which they had disappeared, returned indecisively, stamped and swore. The silly bags were obviously not worth guarding, and as it turned out we were to lose them anyway, yet they weighed on my conscience. Of course I pondered the wisdom of setting off in the rain to comb the cafés, but supposing, as could so easily happen, I lost all contact with him and the ship sailed? After a while the feeling of committal that accrues from having waited for anything won the day. I would not lose my investment and so I waited on.

Brendan had brought three books along with him to

further our literary education, or perhaps to impress the Czech littérateurs: *Gryll Grange*, the second volume of Thackeray's *Pendennis* and Miss Austen's *Mansfield Park*. He still had hopes of the novel as a form. I fished them out of the preposterous suitcase, closed it, sat on it and tried them all in turn.

The rain continued. It blew in gusts over the grey expanse of water in front of me, over the ships, the cranes, the heaps of cargo and under the roof of the shed. I shifted forlornly round the building in search of shelter, moving the suitcase, the grip and the three books with me. Again, for fear of losing contact I dared not go round the back out of sight of the ships and the quays, but of course the back of the shed was the dryest and least windy side. I was wet, cold, hungry and without any alcoholic solace. And I was to remain so for hours. In these circumstances it was perhaps natural that none of the three masterpieces would take. Oddly enough I got most reward from the second volume of *Pendennis,* some interest being stimulated by the attempt to work out what had gone before, a proof of the fact that it is better to plunge *in medias res*.

Still, even *Pendennis* was sticky going, and of course my attempts to read were punctuated by long, anxious lookings, nervous pacings, bitter recriminations. The port of Rouen seemed remarkably idle that day, at least at our part of the docks, perhaps because of the rain, and though the gangway of the 'Irish Scrub' was down and apparently guarded by a French watchman in a beret who sheltered under the lee of the cabin there was little movement aboard. Of course I knew how stupid it was to sit opposite the ship one intended to stow away on, particularly with one's travelling bags, but there was no other shelter within seeing or hailing distance and there I had to remain. Eventually I could see the watchman had begun to take an interest in me, and after I had been sitting there for a couple of hours with my open *Pendennis* he fetched an officer and the two of them had a conclave. It was in my mind to approach them boldly, explain our position and identify and hope for the best. But I did not know what plot Brendan was hatching out, or thought he was hatching out, with the sailors, and I not

47

only feared to spoil his plans and arrangements, but I feared to risk all on an open approach as well. Meanwhile I read, on and off, and the port of Rouen remained idle, and the watchman watched me, and there were occasional extra strong gusts of rain and eddyings of black cloud under the general greyness. Once a couple of blue-trousered workmen came along and stopped and addressed me in French, taking up the questioning from each other impatiently as if my failure to answer in the same language were only a matter of clarity of exposition. They kept it up for a couple of minutes, then, shrugging, offered me a cigarette and went their way.

Eventually the light, what there was of it, faded, and with the fading of the light came Brendan and the sailors. 'Og from a treason tavern rolling home, liquored at every chink.' I looked up from *Pendennis* and saw the three of them coming along beside the crane-tracks in convivial converse. As they neared the ship they parted and the two sailors went up the gangway. Brendan came over to me. He was not only drunk, he was the drunken man of action. He lectured me volubly and hoarsely, impatient that I could not immediately grasp the cleverness of the arrangements he had succeeded in making, as if he had spent a tiring day working out our fortunes while I sat indulgently under the shed reading *Pendennis*.

It appeared that his companions had bought him a lot of booze on the grounds of his being a Dublin man (which I was not) and had eventually agreed to approach the captain on our behalf. They had no doubt it would be a certainty. We were home and dried. But if by any remote chance the captain said no we were to surreptitiously board the ship, which sailed on the tide within a matter of half or three-quarters of an hour.

One of his companions returned to the gangway and beckoned us over. He was none too sober either, but of course none the less earnest or admonitory for that.

'Now talk to him mind. Talk to him. Tell him the whole story. He won't see Irishmen stuck.'

Unfortunately we didn't get talking to him. We were allowed on board all right, observed now not only by the watchman but by two or three other interesed members of the crew, including my friend the officer who stood at the bulwarks with his hands behind his back. With some further admonitions we were then taken by our mentor down a companion-way and as far as the door of what appeared to be the captain's cabin.

On this he knocked, and, being bade to do so, partially entered. He started to say something, but was interrupted by a loud and angry voice within.

'No, I told you,' it said. 'No. It's quite impossible, O'Brien. And I don't want to hear anything at all about it. It's out of the question. I don't want to see them or hear anything at all about the matter. Get them off the ship now immediately.'

And that, with some modifications and stiffenings in response to further pleadings from our friend, was the extent of the captain's parley with us.

O'Brien backed out towards us and closed the door.

'Let him go and fuck himself,' he said quite audibly. 'We'll get you on the ship all right. Wait about twenty minutes and then make a jump for it up forward. I'll give you the office.'

We retreated under watchful eyes down the gangway and retired to one side of our shed, Brendan muttering.

The rain was at last coming to an end, and clouds breaking to let the last light through. Lamps had come on along the quays and on the 'Irish Scrub', making it look more home-like than ever, but its black side seemed a preposterous height.

'Surely to God', I said, 'he's not suggesting that we take a lep at it?'

Brendan turned on me with scorn.

'Even if we do miss our god-damned grip,' he said, 'we can't be much worse off than we are. We'd be as well off drown in the river as starve to death in this awful kip.'

He had no liquor, but the sailors had given him some Afton Major cigarettes. We stood under the roof of the shed and smoked in the gathering darkness while noise and lights and movement on board suggested the ship's imminent departure. Diffidently I argued not only the dangers but the possible indignities of the enterprise, while he with a scorn and confidence induced by many brandies attacked my pusillanimity. According to his story once on board we would be secreted, sheltered and cosseted by the crew, either all the way to Ireland or until such time as the Captain had no option but to let us stay. The leap itself he declared to be little or nothing, even for unfit men such as ourselves.

I had by no means decided one way or the other when we heard a soft shout and saw three figures gesturing at us from forward of the gangway. Brendan tossed his cigarette on the ground, picked up his bag and strode forward with one of his special walks, shoulders back, chest out, legs individually assertive.

O'Brien leaned over the bulwarks, flanked by two companions.

'Jump up here', he said, 'and the next thing you're in the Liffey'.

It was an unfortunate phrase. 'Easier said than fucking done', muttered Brendan, reversing his line somewhat now that we were confronted with the leap and could hear the dark water sucking below. 'Fucking easy for you to talk, up there high and dry.'

'Sling us up them bags', said O'Brien. A little venomously, Brendan threw up the large suitcase and the duffle-bag, narrowly missing our friends' heads with each. I followed, more reluctantly, with the grip.

We were now standing empty-handed, the preliminaries over, face to face with the decision itself. The top of the bulwark was scarcely higher than a man could actually reach if he stretched his arms upward, but of course it was a couple of feet from the quay. All the stretching in the world would be no good. A leap it would have to be. It was not so much drowning as being crushed to death down there between the ship's side and the quay that terrified me, but there was no doubt that if one stood looking at it one would lose all power of leaping.

Brendan jumped, clung, scrambled and was aboard. I was alone with the dreadful decision, cold, empty, sober as a monk at matins. The sawn-off Wellingtons seemed a terrible impediment. I stood back a pace or two and then incompetently flung myself forward and upward. To this day I cannot believe that I made any rational decision to jump. The whole movement was something in the nature of a reflex action. There was a small dark eternity in the void, followed by the wild hope that one half made it as one grabbed, was grabbed and pulled upwards and inwards, levering desperately with elbows, praying that the sailors had the strength to haul and that one's clothes or arm joints would not give way.

I landed in a heap on the deck. Brendan reviled me for making too much noise. A little confusion in my mind as to where we were led by our mentors next I attribute to a reaction produced by the unbelievable risk just run, as well as to the fact that I was now a dumb follower, in everybody's omnipotent hands. We went down some sort of a metal ladder, tricky in itself I remember. There was a short, metal-floored alleyway and then a gap in the side-wall, with a sort of metal threshold to it. Inside that appeared to be a pit of some kind, pitch dark.

'Jump in there', O'Brien said casually. 'Go on. It's only a few feet.'

Christ, I thought, not another jump, but making a bending movement at the knees and swinging his arms like somebody going for a dip on Christmas morning, Brendan disappeared. I heard him land on something that clattered. By now I thoroughly disapproved of the whole operation, but I sat down on the edge, dangled my feet for a moment and then timidly lowered myself in. It was only a few feet and it was coal. A metal door clanged shut behind us. We were now in absolute darkness.

I was at the bottom of a declivity and Brendan appeared to be scrambling up one side of it. I followed him with some displacement of lumps. From where he eventually chose to lie one could touch the roof above us, a most unpleasant feeling. I must say I at once began to complain. I suggested, I am afraid, that we get ourselves out of there immediately, give ourselves up or do whatever was necessary to get ourselves out of it anyway. We knew nothing about the nature of the place we were in. For all we knew we could be tilted mechanically into a furnace without an instant's warning. Or else we could be buried alive under a new influx of coal.

Besides, I argued—and in all honesty I think I can say that this weighed at least equally with me—our situation was now ridiculous. Whatever the merits of arriving back in Dublin after stooping to other forms of stowing away, to arrive back after hiding in a coalhole was to invite nothing but jeers. I pointed out that in my case there would be more humiliation than in his. If we were brought ashore in irons, as was very likely, there would be, in my case, grotesquely humiliating and well-publicised aftermaths to do with my accursed barristership-at-law; that I cared of course nothing for it *per se*, but that I cared greatly for the public indignities it might occasion.

To all this Brendan responded by calling me a Babu member of the middle-classes. It was untrue and it was unfair but he put me on the defensive, as all determined and scurrilous radicals can put counsellors of mere reason and moderation. Intimidated, I forbore to point out that I had been shivering under the shed all day with the respectable Mr. Thackeray's *Pendennis,* while he had been knocking back the *fines et l'eau* and singing his old war-songs with the sailors. It was easy, I felt like saying, for him to see the whole thing as a jaunt.

And I did something eventually of which to this day I know not whether to be ashamed. There were voices and footsteps on metal. The door rasped open. Someone shone a flashlight into our pit, moved the narrow beam round for a few seconds, and went away again without seeing us. There was a conference in low voices. Then the door opened again and a determined voice said, 'Come on out of there'. The light moved round, still without finding us. I had an uncontrollable impulse to make a noise, and I did. I kicked my legs and a quantity of coal rattled down the slope on which we lay. The voice said, more confidently: 'Come on. I know you're there.' The light arced upwards and found us. We lay for a while in its beam, foolishly, as if invisible. Then, shameful relief in my heart, I crawled or slid down the coal and stood up to face the aperture. Reluctantly Brendan followed and we both scrambled out. It was the officer who had gazed at me from the ship. The French watchman stood beside him, displaying the artificially strong amusement with which louts greet discomfiture of any kind.

The officer was not amused but, mercifully, taciturn. He escorted us monosyllabically up on deck. The gangway had been taken in. There was a short delay while it was being run out again. It became evident that we were simply going to be put ashore. Brendan stood beside me, muttering vehement abuse. I had nothing to say, but I nodded agreement several times over while the watchman explained in atrocious English that it was not good policy to sit all day with your valises in sight of the ship on which you were going to try to secrete yourself. To my annoyance, Brendan did not seem to hear.

A small knot of workmen had gathered on the quayside and as we went down the gangway they also thought it proper to display amusement. Brendan told them in English to go and fuck themselves. The gangway was run in again. The engines had started and the ship began to move. O'Brien was leaning over the bulwarks at the stern.

'What'll I do with them bags?' he called.

'Leave them in McDaid's,' said Brendan fiercely. 'McDaid's of Harry Street. Have a drink on me.'

O'Brien threw something at our feet. It was a carton of Afton Major, the recurrent cigarette of our Odyssey. There was now a perceptible distance between the 'Irish Scrub' and the quayside. As she moved out over the dark waters we gave a final wave and turned away. There was nothing else to do.

Shaking off the attentions of the watchman and his friends we walked slowly along the docks. Bitter and prolonged recriminations were the order of the day. Brendan of course had the best of them. They were cut short by the arrival of three or four caped policemen, one with a bicycle. What was said I do not know, but it was evident that they intended to take us in. We made a melancholy little procession as we trudged over the setts and crane tracks in silence. The rain had begun to fall again.

In the police station there were the usual comings and goings. We were made to surrender our passports. Brendan assumed all negotiations into his own hands, a practice which never improved my French. He was somewhat more voluble than the police, but it began to be apparent that they knew nothing of the 'Irish Scrub' and that there was some question of contraband. The carton of Afton Major was opened and examined. We were evidently supposed to have been smuggling cigarettes. Eventually while one of their number busied himself with a telephone, we were made to sit on a wooden form in an outer office.

We continued to sit there for two and a half hours. The recriminations had ceased and we sat mostly in silence. It was now the best part of a day since I had eaten or drunk anything at all. Brendan hunched his shoulders, walked about and glowered. Whatever solace he had been able to avail of with the sailors was evidently losing its glow. The clock ticked on.

Then one of the original party returned and gave us back our Afton Major. We could go, it seemed. Before handing back our passports he had a bit of a laugh about something in one of them with his colleagues.

'What do they think they're laughing at?' I said to Brendan.

'He's explaining what barrister-at-law means', he replied bitterly.

It was late and the streets were deserted. We went aimlessly up a hill towards nowhere in particular. We had our Afton cigarettes, but, it seemed, no matches. At the top of the hill there was a small square, with some demolished buildings and widely spaced lamps. We sat down on the stump of a wall.

Out of a dark patch on the other side a man began to cross over towards us. He was small, blonde, youngish and battered. Brendan got up to ask him for a light. They stood in converse for a few seconds. I could see him examining the strange packet. Then they moved towards me.

'You got nowhere to go eh?' the stranger asked. 'Nowhere to sleep?'

We assented. He looked at us speculatively. 'I fix you up', he said. 'I see you O.K. I got a place.'

We set off. Our companion was wearing a sailor's jacket with one elbow torn. We walked in silence, but it wasn't far.

Down another street were some bombed-out houses. At the door of one he paused. 'You follow me now', he said. 'I light a match.'

We felt our way up a bare wooden staircase. There was that damp burnt smell that clings to bomb-sites. At the top our companion turned. 'You mind now please', he said. 'There is no floor.'

There wasn't. There were only bare burnt joists across which he proceeded to pick his way, one hand on the wall, the other holding an unsteady match. It was impossible to see what lay beneath. When we were half-way over the match went out and the rest of the journey had to be accomplished in the dark, both sweating hands against the plaster, each hesitant step made blindly and slowly by feeling for the next joist. If it had not seemed even more dangerous I would have given up and stood where I was.

Even now it makes me sweat to think of that crossing, but we made it. Beyond a doorway in the further wall was a small room with, mercifully, a floor. We all three sat down on this, there being of course nowhere else to sit, and smoked in the darkness.

Our companion was a seaman and according to him there were many such unemployed and derelict in the port. He was a Finn, a displaced person from Petsamo.

'The Russians have it now', he said. 'But what the hell. They can keep it. I don't want it. They got my mudder and my fader and my sisters and all belong to me and they can sure keep them too.'

After a while he said 'shh' and listened. I could hear no sound, but he seemed nervous. Then he said it again and this time we could all hear someone slowly climbing the stairs.

Whoever it was began to advance softly, as if wearing plimsolls or espadrilles, across the joists in the outer room. The Finn said something under his breath, but he remained sitting down. Then somebody appeared in the doorway, struck a flame from a cigarette-lighter, and peered down at us where we sat against the wall. It was an Arab, a big man, with puffy negroid lips and a scar down my side of his face. By the light of the flame he held, I could see a great deal of the whites of his eyes.

For a few seconds there was no word exchanged. Then the Arab said: 'Hello, fuck-pig. You don't bother to come around to-night? You got company of your own?' He inspected Brendan and myself with the flame held a little lower.

'I am O.K. where I am. I am fine,' the Finn said.

'You got schoosy about your friends', said the Arab. 'You don't come and see them when they expect?'

'I didn't say nothing about seeing you at all to-night', said the Finn.

'You go kiss my big dick', said the Arab. 'You air a li–ar.'

He straightened up. He was holding the lighter in his left hand and had something in his right that was all too likely a knife. The Finn sat quite still and there was no move or word out of Brendan who was carefully, like myself, taking no interest in the proceedings. All the same I hunkered myself cautiously and carefully into a more erect position. It eased the mind to be even a fraction of the way to being on one's feet.

There was a long silence. Whatever was between them, the Arab had the dominance.

'I see you around', said the Finn.

'You see me now, buddy', said the other.

'I ain't got nothing to say to you.'

'I might make you say something.' He laughed. It was a coloured man's tee–hee with a suggestion of obscenity to it. 'And do something too.'

He clicked the lighter off and then on again, tauntingly. 'O.K., little buddy, I see you around', he said and backed out through the doorway. We could hear him making his way over the joists and then down the stairs. We all sat quite still, but the relief was immense.

We lit cigarettes and Brendan offered the Finn a packet, which at least made for conversation. No explanations were offered and none asked for. We talked a while, constrainedly even on Brendan's part; and then, lying or leaning against the wall, we composed ourselves as best we could for sleep. I slept all right, Arabs or no Arabs. It had been a long day's non-journey.

The Finn was awake and smoking when I opened my eyes and Brendan woke at the sound of our voices. Beneath the blackened and charred joists in the outer room was a sheer drop to the cellars, mercifully concealed in darkness the night before. The Finn went over like a practised hand and with a sailor's agility. Brendan and I followed more fearfully, he with a hangover, I with nothing but morning in the stomach. The rain had cleared and the sun was shining.

Brendan, who had worked for a while on a boat owned by Eddie Chapman, now alleged that he possessed a seaman's union card and he canvassed with the Finn the notion of applying to–of all places–the British consulate for help as a distressed British seaman. He even had the initials describing his case, D.B.S., off pat. The Finn did not seem either knowledgeable or enthusiastic. Whatever his own position was in terms of nationality or employability we never discovered. Very likely he had deserted for some reason from a ship. He took us down a hill among some other bombed-out buildings to an open space where more distressed or not distressed seamen were lounging about. Brendan attempted to make enquiries, but their English was for the most part even less than our taciturn friend's. I was somewhat perturbed. If the D.B.S. lark should succeed; if Brendan was offered and accepted passage to a home port, which in view of the fact that he was a prohibited person would seem a foolish thing to do, unless they could fix him up all the way to Ireland, what was to become of me? It was the first time that the disturbing notion of *sauve qui peut* had raised its head. I had certainly no desire to spend the rest of my life in Rouen. However, Brendan eventually remembered that his union card was somewhere on the high seas, in the valise aboard the 'Irish Scrub', and that was the end of that notion. He also disclosed that he had about eighty francs, a relic of some change-pocketing during his day's drinking with the Irish sailors; and handsomely explained that, quarrel or no quarrel, he would have bought a drink the night before if we had come across an open café after we had left the police station. However, all's well that ends well. We said goodbye to the Finn and his friends; bought a litre of wine, some bread and a taste of cheese; and, after we had supped and breakfasted, were restored to good humour with each other.

Why exactly we took the road to Dieppe I cannot now remember. Had I, infected by the idea of *sauve qui peut,* already begun to dally with a notion that I might succeed in boarding the Newhaven boat without a ticket? I honestly do not think so. Brendan certainly had some idea that there might be another Irish boat due there; and though I had no relish for a repetition of the performance at Rouen, it seemed a good idea to keep on the move. As it turned out, we were lucky.

We made our way out of Rouen with the sunlight glistening on the wet cobbles and maledictions for it and all its characteristics on our lips. It was many years later that I noticed its resemblance to Waterford, another Norman city.

Our first attempts to get lifts were failures, but after a while as we were resting by the roadside finishing off our litre, along came a brightly painted gypsy caravan, drawn by a grey horse and driven by a lean-faced, moustached man in a red shirt.

We were in holiday mood and it seemed like a good idea to us both. We stood up; stopped, and the red-shirted man motioned to us to mount. There were three other people inside: an old woman, apparently bed-ridden in the interior, a younger woman, and a gorgeous girl of about seventeen. We discovered that they were a family: grandmother, son, his wife and daughter. They were good people too: frank, hospitable, curious, kindly and cheerful. They offered us soup out of an iron pot, a delicious, still-warm bean and meat stew. We drank a little wine together. Brendan sang a bit and told them about being from Ireland, which they all agreed they knew about and must visit some day. The man sang a few bars of something, softly with his wife. Brendan sang again, after which the old woman and the young girl sang together, the old woman playing a thin sad melody on a gourd-shaped instrument which she took down from the wall beside her.

She lay under a rug on a couch in the cluttered interior, her black eyes shining, and the girl stayed in there too, lowering and raising long eyelashes shyly when one risked a look. The driver's wife sat just inside the front opening, behind myself and her husband, and Brendan sat opposite on a painted chair specially placed for him, relaxed and voluble, in one of his many elements.

I remember thinking as the broad fields rolled slowly by in the bright sunshine and the grey horse ambled on before us that if yesterday had been the sort of sordid farce that only we seemed to get involved in, today was a romantic cliché out of the nicest kind of old-fashioned travel book. Compared to the last few days it was a tiny idyll, and it was not spoiled even when the man and the old woman showed us the G's granded on their arms by the Nazis, for were they not, like ourselves, now safe and warm in the sunshine, and is not that sort of thing, alas, a bonus for the traveller, something to talk about afterwards?

Unfortunately, neither Brendan nor I being George Borrow, nor even Walter Starkie, we weren't asked to stay with them for ever, to marry or share the girl, learn to play the stringed instrument and go wandering for ever on the sunlit roads of Europe. Sometime in the late afternoon the man halted his horse at a side-road, pointed in the direction of Dieppe and indicated that they were turning off on some purposes of their own. Adventures to the adventurous, they say; and perhaps there was even, in our own curious way, something conventional about Brendan and myself.

It took us the rest of the golden afternoon to walk to Dieppe. We still had a little money for wine and bread and we lay in the early evening on a sort of grassy headland overlooking the sea and the town. There remained the problem of where to sleep. In our end, Brendan seemed to feel, should be our beginning. He sought out a priest's house, and, the father being fetched to the door in his soutane, told him the old story about being *on perinage* to Rome. Whether the reverend gentleman understood us to mean that we had only just arrived from England and felt that we should have cleaned ourselves up before we started on our way to see the supreme pontiff, or whether he thought that we were now near enough back home with our blessing still intact and were unlikely to die of exposure I do not know, but he certainly wasn't having any. He informed us coldly that there were hotels in the town. When asked—humbly, with a view of course to a touch—how much they cost he replied that he did not know, *'quelques francs'*, he did not know how many, and shut his hall-door on a vision of lamplight and a smell of soup. The episode brought a wave of nostalgia for the more hospitable curacies of the south.

Still, it was a warm enough evening, with a moon now shining on the sea. We decided that the countryside offered better prospects than the town, bought another litre and strolled back the way we had come. Not far out of town we found a bank covered in deep grass and separated from the road by a ditch. It seemed to offer privacy and comfort without being too remote from the protections of civilisation, so we settled down on the grass with our wine and cigarettes and talked and gazed at the moon. Whatever the morrow brought we were in better heart and better circumstanced than the night before.

The morrow in fact brought an Australian on a bicycle, who was gazing at us from the road as we woke up, and the story of our pilgrimage really ends here. The Australian was a decent fellow and he took us to coffee and croissants in the town. Brendan found out from some dockers that an Irish ship was expected in two days. The Australian, now aware of our predicament, asked us why we did not simply go on board the Newhaven packet. Tickets were not collected until after it sailed and we could give our names to the purser. We explained about Brendan being a prohibited person. The Australian offered us some money—not much, but enough for one for two days. Brendan insisted that I should go. Apart altogether from the fact that I had made a balls-up of the last attempt, he was a Dubb-el-in man. There would be Dubb-el-in men on the ship and they wouldn't see him stuck, though they might view him with less favour if he was in company with a kulchie from the County Wexford. Eventually I decided that I would. The boarding was easy, but when Brendan waved once from the dark quayside then turned away and walked assertively towards a lighted café, I naturally felt that I was abandoning him.

However, he survived. Apparently exercising the prerogatives of a Dubb-el-in man, he got home on that other Irish ship and about a week later I met him in McDaid's.

And so ended The Pilgrimage To Rome, The Flight Behind The Curtain, The Service Under The Tricolour and The Days Before The Mast. Not to mention, it seems to me now in retrospect at least, an era in a relationship. I know that life has a habit of marking transitions of feeling on the calendar in a way that is false. Looking back we associate such transitions with journeys, seasons, public events that have really nothing to do with them. For some time we continued more or less as before, though both of our circumstances were changing and drama, of a sort, was in the offing. But I see him differently as from that time, and certainly most of the rest that I have to tell about Brendan Behan is considerably darker, though it includes the days of the fame that many must have envied. So far as I am concerned, much of what follows is nothing less than nightmare. It is true that I ceased to see the whole picture and did not know the whole story, but much of what I did see is neither pleasant to the memory nor gratifying to the reflective faculty.

4

BRENDAN HAD a voracious appetite for public notice. Wherever he was he sought it out, and usually he got it. He would perform before any sort of audience willing to grant him its attention, even if that audience was, as it frequently turned out to be, uncomprehending, baffled or, occasionally, hostile. One day around this time we had a meal together in the Bailey. It was late lunch-time and we were the only customers in the long bar. For the benefit of a solitary waiter he put on a performance, including song, mimicry and anecdote, which lasted at least half an hour. He was at the top of his form and much of the carry-on was of surpassing brilliance. As we were about to leave he went to the jakes. 'Musha, poor Brendan,' said the patient waiter. 'He's rambling in his talk.'

Up to around the time of our pilgrimage, however, he had been the dominating figure in a circle where, however undiscriminating it was, he at least commanded unlimited admiration. With his republican background, his prison record, his escapades, his verbal fluency and wit, his multifarious and extraordinary talents, he had been a good deal more than just an indulged performer, for he was also forthright, arrogant, exceptionally intelligent and domineering by instinct. Nor were his literary pretensions weighed against his actual achievements by anybody with any real standards. We lived in a sort of loose bohemia where anything got by and almost anything was regarded as a proof of genius. He himself was almost the most literate man around.

Now, however, things began to change. McDaid's itself, the principal *mise en scène* of his triumphs, was changing, as, like all pubs, even it does, within limits. Much of the crowd who had been going there were dispersed. Many were sojourning in England, for economic and other reasons, some even to procure divorces. Others had quietly disappeared, presumably having adjusted themselves to ordinary living, or dropped into darker depths. And from being predominantly bohemian-revolutionary, the pub had become predominantly literary, in fact the headquarters of a literary monthly, *Envoy*.

Unpublished writers are like other over-imaginative people in that they are inclined to think themselves the focus of everybody's attention to a much greater degree than they really are. Consequently they suffer from the notion that everybody is assessing their progress and perhaps commenting on the absence of major works which would justify a certain amount of arrogance, or at any rate indigence and apparent idleness. Brendan was oddly insensitive in several respects, but this was not one of them. He did invite attention. At the same time he suffered from what he thought was surveillance and comment by people who were actually minding their own business. This set up tensions in him when others began to publish and he failed to do so. Unluckily for him also, his position in the new order was complicated in another way.

The dominant figure in the magazine and, latterly, in the pub, was a man of genius, Patrick Kavanagh. At this time in his late forties, Kavanagh had had an unorthodox, troubled and rather unhappy literary history. Born on a farm in Monaghan, he had begun to write poetry in the late nineteen-twenties and early thirties. Discovered by A.E., at that time editor of the *Irish Statesman*, he had been brought to Dublin as a primitive genius from peasant Ireland; in many ways, the latter-day Irish revivalists who then controlled the scene thought, the answer to their prayers. In fact his early poems are rather Georgian, and some of them are nature-struck in a rather literary way, the sort of poems one might expect a highly sensitive countryman who had been rather restricted in his models to write, given burgeoning genius. But they exactly suited his sympathisers and there was quite a prolonged honeymoon with literary Dublin.

63

Kavanagh sat in the Palace Bar, the haunt of journalists and men of letters, and he listened for a long while, entranced. Here at last for him was literary Dublin, in fact the inner circle of the local world of letters, and it appeared to him for the while that he was a part of it. As far as those around him were concerned, he exactly fitted the bill. He was enormous, uncouth, and, to a large extent, unlettered. And his *gaucheries* gave his companions an advantage, which is always a comfort where peasant, or, indeed, any other kind of genius is concerned.

Unfortunately the relationship was based on a misunderstanding. They were, for the most part, suburban literary men, who had been left in comfortable charge of a national literature by the disappearance or default of its progenitors, and they did not want the even tenor of their ways disturbed. Kavanagh, although they did not know it, was potentially a highly explosive force. He was also an actual sophisticate, where they were merely urbane and patronising. Besides, he soon began to feel–to a large extent, justly–aggrieved, for they had the good jobs in the civil service, the radio and the galleries and they had the houses to go with them, while he was forced to bend his talents to unsuitable and ill-paid journalism, like a column of homespun chat under the name Piers Plowman in the *Irish Press*, or the film criticism he did for the *Standard*, a Catholic weekly. Feeling aggrieved, he imagined himself cunning when in fact he was merely being treacherous. A general falling out, with wrong on both sides, was inevitable, and when it came Kavanagh proved, not surprisingly, to have had all along an unclothed intellect and a forceful tongue. His judgements of the locals became less and less tolerant; the ways in which he struck home more intolerable to their self-esteem. They affected to believe for a long time that his summary dismissals of their talents were merely due to a combination of jealousy and lack of good taste, but he made them uncomfortable all the same and they reacted by jeers and ostracism. For a while they would gravely admit to the genius; then, as the poems took on a new and disturbing edge, even that fell into disrepute. Kavanagh was dropped from literary Dublin.

The town, it is true, buzzed with stories of his sayings

64

and his behaviour, but they were stories designed to show him as a clumsy, maladroit, mannerless oaf, and among the sort of people who retailed them, even the now very cursory acknowledgments of genius were left out. One heard such stories everywhere. They were part of Dublin's social currency: the story of how Kavanagh had taken off his boots at the public meeting in Trinity College, what he said about her arse to the titled lady who took him to dinner, his reference to the year he had the bath, his approval of the Country Shop as a place to eat because 'you got your bellyful there, and it was dainty'. It never occurred to anyone that there might be a form of valid social protest in this kind of behaviour, or if it did the uncomfortable thought was quickly suppressed. If the person concerned was literary he might just gravely incline his head and say it was a pity Paddy hadn't stayed down on the farm and stuck to the lyric thing, that he was making a fool out of himself in Dublin and it wasn't doing him any good.

It therefore came as something of a surprise to me, when I met him through *Envoy*, to find that Patrick Kavanagh was a deeply serious man with an intellect which was humorous and agile, as well as being profound and apparently incorruptible. He was also, in that first relationship at least, apparently warm and generous. On somebody who already admired his work his impact was extraordinary. More than any other man I have met, he fitted Doctor Johnson's description of Edmund Burke: 'If you sheltered with him in a doorway from a drove of oxen for a minute, you would depart from him knowing you had been in the company of a man of genius.'

Of course *Envoy* itself had come as a godsend to him. When it came along he was totally without literary friends; jobless, and ostensibly at least–for there were always elements of concealment in his finances–penniless. In the view of his enemies, he had been almost finished. Now he suddenly had a forum where he could speak his mind uninhibitedly and with a good deal of accumulated *saeva indignatio* to give what he had to say resonance. A gregarious man, he had been largely without an ambience, and, except for his locals round Baggot Street, without a pub. Now he had found one where, apart from other matters, he could at least discuss the racing page with the layabouts of Grafton Street and where he could be broke and *non bourgeois* without apologies or aggression. He had been without allies, but *Envoy*, with a little hocus pocus, could be made to sound like the voice of a movement. It was at least internationally minded. It printed expatriate Americans like Donleavy whom he found for the moment less objectionable than the bilingual element in the Pearl Bar. If, on examination, the movement turned out to be an illusion, so do all other movements everywhere and always. There was also, to use his own phrase, a few bob stirring, for, aside from what he was paid officially, John Ryan, who edited the magazine, was, within limits, good for a pound here and a pound there. But, apart from anything else, he had found friends and supporters; and in one or two of us he declared he had found initiates who operated on his own level as far as certain ultimate matters were concerned. 'To think how I wasted these last few years when there were people walking up and down Grafton Street who were ready to be my friends', he said.

Unfortunately for Brendan, he aroused in Kavanagh feelings of loathing and apprehension which are, on the mere face of it, difficult to explain. There was certainly an element of fear in them, for Kavanagh's was a highly developed and sensitive organism that dreaded certain forms of disturbance; and there was perhaps an instinctive recognition on his part of the hysteria latent in Brendan which came to the surface when his claims for attention or affection were denied. If so, he was the first to recognise it. I was to see plenty of it myself later.

Anyway, on Brendan's appearance the huge frame would become visibly agitated. The great shoulders would shake, the enormous hands fidget nervously, the long head swivel from side to side in search of allies or openings; and, unless well protected by company he trusted, the poet would frequently flee into the night. His feelings towards the cause of all this agitation were to become greatly exacerbated by the events of the libel action in which he got himself involved later, and in which the other played a crucial, if somewhat mysterious, part; and of course after Brendan's fame, and, in Kavanagh's opinion, his phoniness became an international matter, they knew no bounds, for Paddy could not stand success of any kind even in the case of those he loved, but they existed from the earliest days of their acquaintance when Brendan should have been to him, one would have thought, no more than a rather noisy fellow trying to capture his attention in a pub. Phony and blackguard were the terms he used oftenest, but later he was to use the word evil and to repeat it with increasing frequency and emphasis. There was, I am afraid, a very definite sense in which each of these terms was applicable.

Fortunately in the early days their contacts were not such as to force any decision about loyalties on their friends. Brendan was away a good deal, either on Eddie Chapman's boat or on the Continent, during the first year or so of their acquaintance, the year Kavanagh became a regular frequenter of the pub, and the rest of the time he was working sporadically as a house-painter. It was well into the following year before a choice was called for on any occasion that I remember, and by then Brendan had largely given up McDaid's for the time being.

By then also he was incurring a loss of popularity all round which affected him for the worse. There were various reasons for this. He was for one thing appallingly well known around Dublin, and in his blue suit and open-necked shirt he was becoming all too familiar a figure. Being essentially a repetitive performer who polished up his pieces as he went along, his stock-in-trade was becoming all too well known also. He would let nobody pass and when he lacked confidence there was an air of rehearsal in his approach and of entrapment about the delivery—almost on the level of 'wait till you hear the latest'—which was off-putting. Many of his comments and witticisms had always been rehearsed, but there had not been such a doggedness about forcing the product on the auditor whatever the circumstances.

For confidence he was now beginning to lack. The Catacombs circle was breaking up and a new note had been introduced into McDaid's which he felt to be hostile. He was suffering badly from non-publication and, as always, his reaction was defensive. He had had two Irish poems and a very short story in the early issues of *Envoy*, but thereafter it did not seem to want anything. I myself had become what was called 'associate editor' of the old *Bell* early in 1951. Sometime in the summer of that year Brendan gave me a wedge of typescript. It was called 'The Bridewell Revisited' and was about his Borstal experiences. It was in fact the first fifty pages or so of what was subsequently to be called *Borstal Boy*. How free an agent Brendan thought I was I do not know. The facts were that although I did all the donkey work for five pounds a week, the editor, Peadar O'Donnell, felt he had to prove his ultimate authority by a system of delphic suggestions and mystifying vetoes. And for some reason the name of Brendan Behan was anathema to him. Somewhere in the not too distant past there had evidently been an encounter of some sort between them. Peadar was an old republican revolutionary too, and the occasion was perhaps a republican commemoration of some sort, perhaps even Bodenstown, with a black-hatted, stern-visaged Peadar receiving the recognition that he felt all too rarely came his way. Then the apparition of a drunken Brendan. The references to the famous piece in *The Bell* heretofore referred to not being received perhaps with sufficient enthusiasm, the literary brotherhood maybe altogether disavowed before their mutual, largely unlettered republican acquaintance, Brendan had probably passed from familiarity to abuse, and Peadar, who hated drink with a fierce puritanical hatred, would have found his vanity, his literary and revolutionary achievements and his rural origins discussed at length by one of the most scurrilous tongues in Europe, and all this on an occasion and at a gathering where he would normally have borne his part with a gravity which cloaked his delight.

Anyway, whatever had passed between them, what was certain was that he did not want Brendan Behan in *The Bell*. I must say that I did not push too hard. Where Peadar was concerned I knew all too readily when I was beaten and in matters more important, as it seemed to me at the time, than Brendan's prison reminiscences, he had me on the defensive. Nor, to tell truth, was I over-enthusiastic about the piece as it then stood. The I.R.A. element of my acquaintance, Brendan included, rarely talked about battles long ago, and, in the version I saw at least, it seemed to me that he was writing a species of Sunday newspaper autobiography. Compared to much else that went into *The Bell* it was doubtless a work of near genius, but I had expected something more and other from him, and our friends suffer from our expectations.

Perhaps I was awkward and inarticulate about the return of the manuscript, but anyway Brendan took its rejection badly, as who wouldn't? He had tried it on *Envoy* also. They too had failed to publish it, and he now, I think, conceived the notion that he was being discriminated against. Later he was to allege that this was on class grounds, that a combination of bogmen and bourgeois were against him because he was a member of the Dublin working class, and he began to feel aggrieved.

The result of his alienation from McDaid's was that he began to go further afield to look for an audience, and to go often into company, perhaps that of a certain kind of Trinity student, or the more raffish type of middle-class lounger who frequented other Grafton Street pubs, which might for a while treat him as a curiosity and a distinctive personality, but ultimately did not understand him at all. This didn't do him any good mentally or socially and he would pass from would-be entertainer to abusive attacker with startling rapidity and unpleasant results. He had taken to carrying the folded wad of typescript round with him as a sort of protest against the pusillanimity of the various editors who had rejected it and as proof of the fact that he had been working, which indeed he had. Whenever one met him one would see it sticking out of the inner pocket of the blue suit. The unfortunate thing about carrying one's works about when one is drinking is the temptation to force them on people's attention. At a certain stage of the proceedings Brendan would in fact begin to read extracts from it to his company, with the result that the wad began to acquire a certain dreaded notoriety which was in sad and ironic contrast to the fame the finished book was to win for itself later on.

The years from now until the first production of *The*

Quare Fellow and his subsequent marriage were to be, in general, bad ones for him, and as a consequence of the rejections he suffered—some of them self-invited—he began to behave in distressing and obsessional ways. He could not take no for an answer and confronted by a rejection or coldness of any sort he would react with an extraordinary verbal violence, shouting abuse and not infrequently foaming at the lips. His victories depended either on the other party's terror at the spectacle of rage he then presented, or on their mere embarrassment at the degree of noise created and the kind of public attention attracted. Since a Dublin pub audience is highly pleased to have a public show of any kind put on for its benefit, Brendan could depend on their encouragement for the discomforture of the victim, who could only cower or scarper, thus leaving him the field and, in that sense at least, the victory.

He had certain terms of abuse, the damaging significance of which was known only to himself. But since the bystanders cared only for the show he did not have to be too accurate or witty, though of course he was frequently these things too. One of Brendan's special prides, amounting almost to an obsession, was the fact that he was a Dubliner. All those who had the bad taste to be born elsewhere were 'Kulchies'—called so of course after the town of Kiltimagh, pronounced Kulchimah, in County Mayo—or bogmen, because of the prevalence of bogs in rural Ireland. They were supposed to possess traits of character, particularly avarice and cunning, from which those born in the slums of Dublin were singularly free. Kavanagh, the peasant poet, the archetypal country-man, was to become a special target for this line of abuse; and because his long poem *The Great Hunger* was concerned with sexual frustration in rural Ireland and its symbolic countryman, Maguire, occasionally masturbated, he became without any justification other than a work of the imagina-tion—a common process—'the Monaghan wanker' and was eventually so referred to in the Paris little magazine *Points*, where one of Brendan's few published pieces dating from this time appeared. (The issue of *Points*, with its bright yellow cover, became in the end almost as familiar as the typescript.) Hailing from the County Wexford as I did, I too was finally a Kulchie, though in fact Wexford is as different from the County Mayo as Berkshire is from Banff.

But I go ahead of my story. In spite of 'The Bridewell Revisited' and other matters, our relationship had by no means foundered. We had a quarrel or two, but they passed over. His obsession with Kavanagh and his attempts to force himself on his notice had not yet grown to the pitch they were to arrive at later—there was as yet no ranting in the streets—and if we were no longer daily companions we continued to associate companionably enough.

He was not, it is true, as much fun to be with as he once had been, but he was not unconversable, as he was to become. I had left 'The Gurriers' and moved into a room in a house in Hatch Street. It was a bare enough apartment, with only a stretcher bed and a table and some books, but it was of noble Georgian proportions. When Brendan stayed, as he still did sometimes, he slept in a sort of nest of old newspapers in a corner, and unless Peadar was on the phone editing *The Bell* we still issued forth together in the mornings to see what the day might offer, much as we had always done.

One incident from this time I remember, though whether it is evidence of the general frustrations he was suffering, or of the fact that his principles remained uncorrupted throughout, I cannot say.

It was Christmas, and we came out of McDaid's about nine o'clock to find that it was raining. The Christmas lights were on in Grafton Street, there were more people than usual about, and a bunch of carol singers was standing at the corner with coat collars turned up, still sweetening the damp night air.

They carried placards advertising their charitable intent—something to do with the St. Vincent de Paul Society, or the Legion of Mary or the Morning Star hostel for down-and-outs. As we stood in the rain deliberating the next move, Brendan began to mutter. As I have said, he had in those days a ferocious hatred of the Catholic Church in all its manifestations. We decided to go to Keogh's, which is in Anne Street, and moved towards the corner. The carol singers were still hard at it, tenor and alto, bass and treble, but as we passed them Brendan suddenly seized one of the placards and proceeded to tear up the cardboard and smash the lath while roaring 'Chairman Mao Tse Tung will soon put a stop to your fucking gallop, ye creepin' Jesus's ye.' The singing ended on various notes while he flung the fragments across the road towards Mooney's, bellowing away. There was a moment's hiatus, everybody, including myself, being taken by surprise, and then a couple of by-standers rushed him. He was off like a hare, up Grafton Street and towards Stephen's Green, with about four fellows after him. Fear lends wings to the feet and Brendan kept his distance. At the top of the street he dashed into the roadway and succeeded in gaining the far side well ahead, the others having followed with more respect for the traffic. I crossed over too, but with even more circumspection. Brendan pounded on towards the Harcourt Street end.

The inner side of Stephen's Green was in those days lit by ordinary street lamps and there were pools of light with intervals of darkness in between. The pursuers ran on until suddenly it was evident that there was no quarry in front, then stopped unevenly, regrouped and began to argue among themselves. I stopped too. It was, as Brendan would say, the best of my play. After peering into the bushes inside the railings, they began to straggle back and, hoping not to be identified as the companion of the atheistic communist, I went on and even met them, walking as casually as I could, though of course in fear and trembling. They were still hotly debating and occasionally peering, so I passed unrecognised, whistling a little tune.

I had almost reached the far corner when I heard my name called. It was Brendan, crouching inside under a dripping laurel bush.

'Did you climb those railings?' I asked in surprise.

'Of course I did. Why wouldn't I? Didn't I fucking paint them?' he answered petulantly.

I had to be content with the logic, though it was an astonishing feat to have swung himself over in a dark interval and in the time available.

'Well you'd better climb out again now,' I said, 'because I badly need a drink.'

He climbed over, this time with, it seemed, immense difficulty, and blowing like a grampus. I watched, powerless to aid or hinder, until at last he dropped down beside me. We had both forgotten by then about the outraged populace.

Suddenly there was a rush of feet from quite close by and a shout of, 'There he is, the rotten bastard.' Brendan was off again, this time towards the Russell Hotel, but they caught us in the middle of the road. There was nothing for it but to turn and fight.

Whether it was the shock of our sudden *volte face* or not, after a few rather ineffectual punches were exchanged they gave ground before us, and I learned again what a little determination will do in a fight, a thing an intellectual is always, alas, inclined to forget. In the confusion we got up the steps of the Russell and burst into the lobby on top of a startled porter and some guests.

'There's a mob out there,' shouted Brendan, already beginning to bolt the glass panelled door. The surprised porter came over to have a look for himself. There were in fact four fellows standing outside on the pavement, gesticulating and shouting, but apparently regarding the hotel as some sort of sanctuary, and uncertain as to what to do next.

'Get the rozzers,' said Brendan in tones of command. 'I'm a Dubbelin man. I'm a citizen of no mean city and I'll show these bogmen that there's law and order in this town.'

By the time a police-car arrived the mob of four had apparently given up hope of getting us and drifted off. Brendan told the sergeant he had been attacked for no reason at all in the streets of his own city by a crowd of murderous countrymen he didn't know but suspected to be members of a rural-based organisation of fascist tendencies.

Unimpressed, but equally incurious, the police drove us round the Green and dropped us at the corner of Merrion Row. We went to O'Neill's. Brendan expressed no word of apology, remorse or regret, but he seemed a bit shifty, and at one stage he flattered me by saying 'You're handy with your dukes', which, like all successful flattery, attributed to the opposite party an aptitude he did not possess but would like to.

He stayed that night in Hatch Street and the following morning we found ourselves, not for the first time, broke on Christmas day. We made one or two fruitless visits and then decided to call on a friend who lived in Waterloo Road. After a long wait in the cold we got on a number ten bus and there, sunk in gloom, we found a solitary Patrick Kavanagh. Such was his degree of self-pity that he even failed to get upset at the sight of Brendan. 'I woke up this morning,' he said. 'And what morning was it? It was Christmas morning, the morning of joy, the birthday of the Prince of Peace. "No war, nor battle's sound, was heard the world around, The idle spear and shield were high up hung." And what had I in the house? I had a stale herring from yesterday, a stale uneatable herring. But there was the telephone, fully connected, and ready, you would surely to God and in the name of the Prince of Peace think, to ring. But was there one person in the whole wide city of Dublin who would ring me up to ask me how I was making out and maybe ask me to spend the holy Christmastide with them? There was not. I waited there on my lonesome in the cold for hours and eventually I had to get on the blower myself to a blackguard I know. On this day of all days it's essential to drown your sorrows. I know what I'm in for. It's the worst day in the year and it brings out the bollocks in everybody. But I'll risk it for the sake of a drink.'

We commiserated suitably and crept down the stairs. There on the platform, swaying like a battle ship in a heavy sea, stood an acquaintance of ours who was universally known as 'Tiddely-pip-now' from a form of valediction he was fond of. He was a well-known character, indeed a former footballer and an old republican to boot. His wife had a small business and he himself was rarely known to chance a day's work. On this occasion he was already very drunk and he too wanted to give his views about what he chose to call the Yuletide. 'A lot of people have no time for it,' he said. 'But you can say what you like, it's a day when nearly everybody is happy, a great day for the children and the old, and a day when old quarrels are patched up and old friends reconciled. I'm on my way now to see an old butty of mine I haven't seen for twenty years. He rang me up this morning and asked me round for a few jars. And we'll have a few jars. We'll have a few jars, but I'll be home then for the turkey with the holy help of God.'

Much struck by the contrast in attitude and circumstance we dismounted. Fortunately our own butty had a bottle of brandy in the house and over it Brendan created a Dublin Christmas Carol in which Tiddely-pip was the ghost of Christmas past and Kavanagh the spirit of the starker Christmas present.

Kavanagh lived at this time on the first floor of a house in Pembroke Road, an open, airy, tree-lined Victorian thoroughfare, characterised as a 'jungle' in one of his poems. The end of Baggot Street that runs into it had then three tolerable pubs, one bookmaker's shop and a bookshop. This was his *querencia*. Here he prowled, newspapers under arm, eyes baleful behind horn-rimmed glasses, the enormous hands projecting behind each elbow, hat on head. Often as he walked he talked to himself or, scowling, muttered at the ground. In the local pubs he was well known to all and sundry, and he conversed with everyone whether they would or no, but usually with their consent, for he had views and knowledge on every subject, the more trivial the better. Seldom can there have been such a small area so patrolled by genius: every gurrier in Kilmartin's the bookies, every dart-playing docker in Tommy Ryan's, every gin-drinking landlady or middle-class soak in the Waterloo Lounge was known to him. The girls in the shops and the students and typists who had flats in Pembroke Road he conversed with; indeed he held curious flirtations with many of them, which were nonetheless intense for being merely a matter of street-corner conversation, often mystifying to the girls, about matters ranging from their progress in examinations to the persecutions he suffered.

A broad flight of steps led up to the hall door of the house in which he had his flat and inside the window of the front room he had a driving mirror mounted so that it commanded a view of whoever was ringing the bell. It was a mark of intimacy to be admitted here for whatever reason and the

first time I was invited back was to signalise almost symbolically our common status as outsiders in the company of the
rich. We had been with the Cusacks and Patrick Swift after
the annual exhibition of Living Art. Swift's four paintings
had been the talking point of the show and after a couple of
hours' drinking Cusack asked him and his girl to dinner,
but did not include Kavanagh or myself in the invitation.
We were left in fact drinkless and hungry, so we walked
back through the summer evening to the flat in Pembroke
Road where, as the sky flared outside the big uncurtained
windows, he provided me with black tea and dry bread
and I saw for the first time the battered sofa, the old newspapers, books and yellowing typescripts scattered over the
floor, the tea-leaves in the bath, the mountain of ash that
spilled out of the grate. I asked him, rather stupidly, did he
usually cook for himself, and he answered: 'I sometimes boil
an egg in the teapot, if you call that cooking.'

He spoke, for some reason, of *Moby Dick*, and he fished
out of some place his own much-thumbed copy. Frank
O'Connor, 'a sharp fellow', had recommended Melville to
him. 'He said I'd like him because we were both originals.'
Melville had 'the true Parnassian note. Godlike. Both passionate and uncaring at the same time.' He said the flat was
his incubus. He'd be better off without it and yet he struggled
all the time to hold on, though often in arrears with the
rent. Once the electricity people had dug up the road outside because they couldn't gain entrance to cut him off. He
had offered the workmen cups of tea. Dublin, he said, was
the cruellest city on the face of the earth because Dublin led
you on. A city should ignore you, like London did, which
gave you the English cold shoulder. A city should be im-
personal, but Dublin was full of warm promises, like the
worst kind of woman. If he had stayed in London in 1938
he would have conquered it by now. 'In fact they'd be
setting competitions about me to-day in the *New Statesman*.'

The London venture had been at the time of the publication of *The Green Fool*, 'a ridiculous book by a bollocks. A
bollocks who knew nothing about himself, let alone anybody else.' *Tarry Flynn* was a different kettle of fish. It had
never got its due from anybody, because it didn't contain

Patrick Kavanagh.

the sociological lie, as *The Great Hunger* did. The popularity of *The Great Hunger*, such as it was, was entirely due to the fact that it told 'the sociological lie, the public lie, like Spender and Day Lewis.' He had a soft spot for *Tarry Flynn*, 'which told very little lies.'

In those days the *Envoy* office in Grafton Street was a great place of resort. You climbed up a stairs beside a fish shop (there was always a faint smell of fish hanging about) and eventually you came to a room where galley proofs hung on the wall and there were bundles of the magazine on the floor. There was nearly always company and attendant possibilities, whether for monetary advancement or amusement or both. There were occasional visitors from abroad, writers or aspirant writers. There might be an American girl or two.

Kavanagh would peer round the door at about twelve o'clock, having read–'gutted', as he said–the morning paper and visited one or two of his locals. Though not officially the editor of the magazine he read all the morning mail and interested himself in all the contributions that came in the post, pontificating about them, and, in fact, with whatever concealments, evasions and exaggerations he chose to employ, contributing the intangible quality called life to the whole proceedings. It was a quality I was sorely to miss down in *The Bell*. *Envoy* was an annexe to the pub, or the pub to it. It had an air of gaiety, indeed of conspiracy about it. *The Bell* had not. Nobody I knew seemed to read it and hardly anybody I wanted to see came to the office. There was not a proper pub anywhere in O'Connell Street.

Around one o'clock those in the office would move over to McDaid's. Kavanagh drank stout in those days as a staple and was seldom drunk, or at least any drunker than the rest of us. He was able to go through the day until evening closing time, did not disdain the car journey to Matt Smith's or other pubs in the foothills for the hour and a half or so of licensed drinking permitted to those who were allegedly 'bona fide' travellers; and indeed would often consent to come on to John Ryan's house in Orwell Road afterwards, where he would lie on the floor with his hat over his eyes listening to what was going on and replying cheerfully, when questioned about his well-being or his desire to sleep, 'Don't mind me. I'm only resting. I'm enjoying myself.'

This long haul would have been inconceivable in later years when the whiskey had become his master and was cracking the whip. In a few years his bedtime had advanced to eight or nine o'clock and, before his death, drunkenness, in one form or another, had become his habitual state. What I have to tell about Kavanagh occupies about sixteen years. In them, drink was to advance from being a concomitant to living to being, more or less, its be-all and end-all. The whiskey-drinking began under the aegis of a mutual friend of ours, as decent a man, where drink is concerned, as ever stood in a shoe, during what were for Kavanagh the bad years of nineteen-fifty-three and fifty-four, the years of the libel action and undiagnosed cancer. Unfortunately he proved an addict of a ferocious order and unfortunately also he eventually began to take nightly fistfuls of barbiturates as well, and was subject to the full gamut of illusions and disorders the combination can be trusted to produce.

But all this was in the future in those days in nineteen-fifty and fifty-one when the lunchtime session in McDaid's followed the mornings in the office. There was little whiskey bought then and he had no money to buy it for himself, though he was not for the moment as badly off as he was to become. While *Envoy* lasted there was company. John Ryan or somebody else bought the drink and he sometimes also provided a meal during the holy hour across the road in the Monument café. The drinking with luck would go on through some part of the afternoon and Paddy might then borrow something to go home with, travelling up Baggot Street at a half-run with his head down. It was the years immediately afterwards that he meant when he said that he frequently had to stop people in the street and ask for a shilling for the gas when what he wanted was a shilling for a loaf.

He had during this period also one or two women friends who looked after him to varying extents. One in particular, a Protestant girl descended from one of Ireland's better attested Royal lines, was especially generous, and she also seemed to give him good advice. Her advice was generally quoted as that of a 'friend of mine', or even 'a Protestant friend of mine', but it was usually fairly easy to distinguish her voice from others. His relationship with women, though, had always an air of mystery attached to it—as whose really has not?—only one thing being clear, which was that he looked on them primarily as providers.

Indeed the myth of the rich woman occupied his thoughts to an inordinate degree. Of course the idea of woman as the provider, comforter and arranger of circumstance is common enough among artists of a certain disposition; and there is of course nothing wrong with it: it is the myth of Ceres, Demeter, the moon, the ancient mother goddess of Mediterranean man and various other considerate females and mothers, whether goddesses or no. And indeed the woman with money of her own has frequently provided a happy solution for artists who were unable to earn any, but had status and dignity enough otherwise. It was in fact particularly strong in the years with which I am now dealing. Dylan Thomas made no secret of the fact that he had it too, and the velvet accents of female America were associated in many people's minds with possibilities of monetary support to an extent not always warranted by the facts. But Paddy had it to an obsessional degree. This may have been in part because he apparently had a very strong and capable mother who was able to manage circumstance when no one else could or would. Anyway, it is certainly not too much to say that a good deal of the warmth he felt for women was based on their ability to provide circumstantial comfort of one kind or another.

Money and its possibilities are of course extensions of personality and it is a foolish woman who, being able to alleviate circumstance a little, distrusts the affection she gains therefrom. That Paddy had close and rewarding friendships with women there is no doubt, and he certainly also had one or two violent and hopeless romantic attachments, but he did tend to see women as part of their general monetary ambience and as the centre of a warm penumbra into which he might enter. More luck to those women who were aware of this.

As a result, however, of *The Great Hunger*, some other

poems about sexual frustration, and the prevalent Dublin assumptions about rural bachelordom, he had an extra-ordinary reputation for unwilling virginity around the town, resulting in many allegedly factual anecdotes about situations produced by a combination of desire and naïvety, some of them retailed by suburban literary men who might be married but whose own sexual experiences were, to say the least, limited. One of his best known poems was the quatrain:

> To be a poet and not know the trade,
> To be a lover and repel all women,
> Twin ironies by which great saints are made,
> The agonising pincer jaws of heaven.

This of course was held to be a factual declaration of his dilemma. Also, he paid the usual penalty for having intro-duced a new aspect of humanity's sexual nature into literature –that of being branded as the practitioner, perhaps the sole practitioner, of what he described. Masturbation was one of the themes of *The Great Hunger*. Leaving out *Ulysses*, it was a new theme in 1938. It is hardly so any longer–certainly not after Philip Roth. The fact that it was there in the poem was held to be proof-positive of the assumptions that were made about him. Behan's jibe about the Monaghan wanker was no more than common Dublin currency. The poet in semi-literate societies, such as the generality of Dublin is, needs, alas, to beware of the myth-making powers of poetry.

One evening in McDaid's someone began to quote the verse above. Kavanagh got very angry. 'It's absolute balder-dash', he said. 'It was written when I thought I couldn't get a woman. Now I know it's a damn sight worse to have too many of them.' Be that as it may, his powers of attraction were certainly sufficient to ensure that he got a great deal of what Balzac, after all, called 'the chief consolation of genius', the company and conversation of beautiful women. Looking back on the way Dublin tongues commonly wagged about him in the days before our acquaintance–including some which speak of him now in almost daily reverence–I am astonished that such a caricature could have been created of

81

a living being in such a small place, but then malice, like love, is a wonder-worker; and it was largely not until he had the freedom of his *Envoy* prose Diary and the backing of one or two irreverent spirits in that context that Paddy revealed himself as the truly sophisticated human being that he was. Poetry, for all but one reader in fifty, only occludes things and leaves them open to graver misinterpretation than ever.

Not all of his confidantes were perhaps beautiful, but I remember some who certainly were. I first became aware of him to recognise at a distance when he was courting (if that is the word) the dark-haired beauty who now finally inhabits the song, 'On Raglan Road'. One would see them walking along the street or drinking coffee in Mitchels together; and because I was in digs at the time with her almost equally beautiful cousins I heard more comment about it than I would perhaps otherwise, though it is only fair to say that the whole relationship seemed to be a mystery to the girls too, She would have been, I suppose, twenty years younger than he, and in so far as a man of deep and vulnerable sensibility can be said to have such, probably the great love of his life, but there were others afterwards who were young, fair and amiable enough at least to accompany him to places of public resort and listen to his woes. One at least occupied a special place, and she married a politician too.

Altogether, in terms of the company and conversation of women and the proofs of affection and understanding he required, he didn't do too badly, even at the worst of times. By comparison with the accepted idea of his relationship with the opposite sex in those years and indeed by comparison with the love-life of most of the people who adopted the Monaghan virgin line, his private life was that of a pampered and indulged figure in what almost amounted to a harem. That he never married his rich woman was perhaps due to the very intensity with which the idea was cherished, for such intensities are in everything, but particularly in the relationship of the sexes, self-defeating. It may also have been due to an ultimate romanticism which required an unattainable beauty for its object. He used to distinguish in his cups between 'women for pleasure and women for use'. This was a mere boast, but perhaps it concealed a more important dichotomy of feeling. There were women for being fond of and women for loving, and loving may have been a very remote and sacred ceremony to be performed before a very high and secret altar.

What made the sympathy he contrived to elicit among women in those years the more remarkable was that his local reputation was as much that of an awkward and unmannerly customer who presumed too much on his talent as it was that of the vatic poet. Such is human nature's remarkable power of imagining things that in some way suit it, that I remember hearing before I met him a full description of how he smelled. Indeed I have heard the same allegation in latter days. He was highly unconventional in matters of personal hygiene, as Irishmen and those who dislike cant and hypocrisy tend to be, and as was that great Englishman Doctor Johnson, who had 'no great fondness for clean linen', but he certainly did not smell and in fact he was always fairly clean-looking and generally, like many others of us, took care to wear shirts that did not show the dirt.

His reputation at this time was almost entirely confined to Ireland, but he yearned for London, and he invested that great and complex city with an esteem for letters somewhat beyond its collective deserts. In those years he had been represented in only one English anthology and he was inordinately pleased when, sometime in the early fifties, he was included in *The Faber Book of Twentieth Century Verse*. Though he was almost totally unknown there and, except for those inclusions, his books and a couple of pieces in *Horizon*, unpublished, London became the mythological counter world to Dublin in his thoughts, the hemisphere where the balance of what he knew was redressed. He would speak familiarly of Betjeman, 'Victor' Pritchett and Connolly; he would retail over and over again the story of a lunch with Maurice Macmillan at Boodles (or was it Whites?); he would tell small anecdotes designed to illustrate the superiority of the English over the Irish in matters of taste and judgment; and he would use, in so far as he knew anything about it, the complex, cultural-historical relationship of the English upper classes with their literature as a stick to beat the natives with. This, as a line, suited me; and more or less by default it was made to suit *Envoy*. There was of course an element of comedy in his mythologisings and though I was aware that his name was more or less unknown in England I did not quite realise the extent of the illusion he was trying to create, for himself and for others on the local scene. Of course he was really conducting a very distant love-affair with an organism that existed only in his own imagination; and, like many lovers who create their own illusion, he was creating a comedy of errors, as indeed he was to discover.

For the moment, however, on the local scene he had company and converse: some of it of an order he had not known before, in terms of youth, a sort of freedom and a sort of energy of attack. He had also a weapon to his hand, which could be used in pursuit of what can only be called his political ambitions, for like many Irish poets he had an idea knocking round in his head that there was a sort of arch-poet position which only one man could occupy, that being of course himself. To this shadowy laureateship, somehow acknowledged by the popular voice, although of course the popular voice was also denied all right of election, all others were pretenders, and it was essential that they should be destroyed. There may be something ancestral about this Irish belief in a chimerical distinction, a ghostly crown of laurel which only one man can wear. Certainly the position of Ard Fhile was once a locally acknowledged one, in so far as the ruler of each petty kingdom had a particular poet to his right hand, but the dominance that Yeats exercised when Paddy and his contemporaries were growing up was real and must have lent substance to the illusion that there was still a post to be occupied. In any case, most of Paddy's critical endeavours, indeed a great proportion of his waking thoughts, were devoted to the destruction of those among his contemporaries who had achieved any sort of equivalent local prominence and the prose he wrote in *Envoy* had almost entirely this end in view. There is, I can see on reflection now, something infinitely comic and grotesque about the idea of a battered, penniless and jobless man, and a

84

man of enormous range, imaginative sympathy and talent, spending so much time and energy on the pursuit of a crown which did not exist, and on the discomfiture of the fellow-writers with whom he chose to swop hatreds, but then is not much of Irish history made up of pretenders' quarrels, the incomprehensible vendettas of broken, propertyless men, who had only their hatreds and their protocols to keep them warm?

At the time, personal affection, the intoxication of the daily company of genius and, I might add, the zest for combat, concealed much from me, including the fact that Paddy's jealousies and fears extended also to his friends and allies, that he would 'bear like the Turk no brother near the throne', that he was happiest with a certain sort of mediocrity or with the conversable but largely unpublished young (of which ilk I was the first he had encountered) and that at the slightest sign of distinction, or even, to put it now bluntly, the sort of poetic achievement he could not interiorly deny, paranoia would come uppermost immediately. But how was one to know that then, and would one have been any happier if one had?

He had, it must be said, however, good reasons for adopting some of the attitudes that he did to the scene around him and for regarding the more comfortable dispositions that others seemed able to make of their very much lesser talents and their lives with envy and even rage. Certainly, consolations of genius aside, his situation was an appalling one for a middle-aged man who had contributed deeply to the unformulated consciousness of his country and his race.

He was writing very little verse, except as afterthoughts to the *Envoy* Diaries, and had not written much in the previous five years. He was probably suffering from an inability to get the man he had become, defeated and angry, but humorous as well, detached, indeed anarchic, but strangely full of hope at the same time, into the poems. The breakthrough came some time after I went to *The Bell*.

He had begun to hate solemnity and mere lyricism. He enjoyed the trivial comedy of the pubs and Kilmartin's; he hated fraud; but the poems up to now had mostly been lyrical remembrances of country living, contrasted in a rather too easy way with his later disillusion and circumstances. It was after I went to *The Bell* that with a new kind of confidence and carelessness, Kavanagh the city poet was born; and he began to produce poems in a direct, conversational manner with ironic undertones, which used Pembroke Road, the flat, the bookmakers, the days he spent, either as themes or images; and which were written in something approaching the conversational manner of the living man, with a sort of humorous but tender advertance to the fact that they were being written at all and that they were poetry. 'Auditors In', 'Intimate Parnassus', 'On First Looking into E. V. Rieu's Homer', 'Surely My God is Feminine' and many others. in fact most of the poems contained in the volume *Kitty Stobling* were published in *The Bell* under my editorship. They were the first products of Kavanagh's late maturing, the first examples of the kind of poetry that made him important; and if I mention the matter now it is partly to put the record straight and partly because my opinion of myself as an editor was not very high, nor, dear knows, was I encouraged on any side to take a much higher one than I did, so that I look back now with a sort of bemused wonder on the strange excellencies of many of the things that actually did get into the magazine.

Eventually I arrived at an arrangement with Peadar whereby Paddy whould be paid cash on the nail for every poem he produced, the sum involved usually being a fiver. It is extraordinary what this can do to the mechanism of those in need, even in the case of a vagrant and delicate matter like the writing of poems. The compact involved extensive use of the telephone, an instrument of which Paddy was inordinately fond. When ensconced at home with the telephone, and, in later years at least, perhaps a drink beside him, he paid no attention whatever to the other party's situation, whether they were in an office, a noisy pub or a drafty telephone booth. The conversation rambled on at his dictation, whether the other party liked it or not. He would telephone me most mornings anyway, but if he had written anything and wanted the money, he would continue to ring at intervals until Peadar showed up. The office was a tiny one, and sometimes Peadar would have arrived before he rang again. 'Any sign of him yet?' he would ask while I pressed the instrument closer to my ear, and then he would go on, oblivious of all signals, to deliver his opinion of his benefactor.

He was fond of quoting, or rather, misquoting Goethe: 'Beware of what you want in youth, for you'll get it in middle-age', he would say, presumably thinking of how he had yearned in Monaghan for recognition in literary Dublin. Now he had it; but both in form and in ancillary circumstance it was grotesquely different from his imaginings. Actually he had the sort of youthfulness that comes only in middle-age, youth itself being full of lethargies and despairs, but he had, all the same, an acute sense of the passage of time, and he used to quote Marcus Aurelius to the effect that as one got older oneself the crowd in the street remained the same age. Once I accompanied him down to the *Irish Press* where he was collecting a small cheque for one of the many anonymous contributions he made to a little feature on the sports page called 'Sporting Prints'. As always when one is on the receiving end of money there was a delay, and we stood on the steps outside while we waited. In front of us there was a man for some reason unloading iron bars from a lorry. Kavanagh began to discourse to him about the fulcrum or the point of balance. After a while the man said: 'I have three lorries on the road and I'm not thirty-five years of age yet.'

'You're a highly insensitive fellow', Kavanagh replied. 'On the eve of my seventeenth birthday, a beautiful night with a full moon shining, I wrote a poem lamenting that life had passed me by and that I had achieved nothing.'

Like Samuel Johnson he was interested in all technical processes and in all human procedures and he would engage any man in conversation about his own speciality. Racing occupied many hours of his day. He delighted in the technical jargon here, which he used figuratively and ironically in any context. 'He'll be running on gamely up the hill when a lot of the others will have had enough', he said of a certain writer, and of another, 'He's only an old handicapper. What we want are classic prospects.'

He had begun to back horses the year Nimbus won the

Derby, which would have been about two years before I met him. Apparently he had been walking along Merrion Row when he met an unnamed friend. It was outside Messervy's the bookmakers and the friend told him it was Derby day and that he was going to back a horse. Paddy enquired the name of the animal and was told, 'Nimbus', which for some reason pleased him. He went in with his friend, found out the procedure and had five shillings on it himself. Of course it won, and he was hooked. From then until his death seventeen years later he backed horses every day and everything connected with the sport became, with whatever ironies, part of his mythology. He used to tell me that I was too reasonable a punter. 'It's a Dionysiac activity– Apollo has nothing to do with it', he would declare. He used the fact that he was a habitual punter often to conceal his assets. If he was discovered to have money he would say he had won it; if he was believed to have it and was pretending to be broke he would say he had lost it. Often humorous references to racing would appear in the poems, to the mystification of the uninitiated: thus the stretch of pavement, on which he had so many adventures, from where he lived up to Baggot Street Bridge, became the Rowley Mile, after the famous straight course at Newmarket. He was full of superstitions. It might adversely affect the result of a race if he stayed in the bookmakers while it came in. He would therefore walk to the pub or the corner and then, when he was sure all was over, return. Anyone who gratuitously informed him of the result as he came back to see for himself would be the victim of his wrath and often held in some way responsiblefor his unsuccess. If he stepped on the cracks between the paving stones while he returned that could have an influence too, although of course the result had already been decided.

In the early days of our acquaintance he did not actually go racing very much. That came later. When he did go, it was like almost everything else, even his way of entering a pub, in which every move and word was calculated for maximum effect from the time he peered round the door to the time he reached the counter, a performance. He would lie stretched out on the lawn in front of the members' stand at the Phoenix Park with his hands behind his head, his hat over his eyes and his legs crossed, looking for all the world like Marc Chagall's *Poète Elongé,* and he would sometimes maintain this posture even while a race was run. Towards the end he affected a great weariness of manner and spirit, and he would often flop down on a bench and sit there with his knees spread, his head bowed and his joined hands deep between his legs. There was a bench under the hedge beside the paddock at the Phoenix Park where you could sit and see the horses come out. At the close of his days W. T. Cosgrave, the former President of the Executive Council of the Free State, would often sit there, with his umbrella between his knees and his hands crossed on top of it, an old man in the sun, his work behind him, watching the two-year-olds. One day Paddy was sitting there when W. T. came along and sat down also. They sat in silence for a while, resting in their different ways, variously weary in spirit, but solaced by their surroundings. Then Paddy spoke.

'Forgive me for intruding, Mr. Cosgrave', he said. 'I know all about intrusion. People are constantly intruding on me, in pubs and everywhere else, and I know how evil it is. But I would just like to tell you that I have admired you all my life. You're a gentleman.'

At this point, much to Paddy's surprise and delight, W. T. turned to him and said: 'Ah, Mr. Kavanagh. I know your work of course and I admire it very much. It's no intrusion at all, I assure you. It gives me great pleasure to meet you.' Whereupon the two shook hands, and having no further need for communication, lapsed into silence.

One of the keenest pleasures he got out of backing was the indulgence of the contempt in which he held other punters. He learned of the philosopher A. N. Whitehead's concept of 'negative prehension' from the Auden poem in which it is celebrated. Misunderstanding the phrase, Kavanagh declared that 'negative prehension' was the key. Whatever the tipsters said, whatever was consensus of opinion among other punters, must be wrong. One backed another horse.

There was at one time a somewhat elderly and habitually rather bemused barman in McDaid's whose name was John.

He was very slow in movement, more than a little deaf and had the petulance of the aged, so, roar though he might, Kavanagh did not always get served as promptly as he would have liked. Because of the white hair he decided to call this barman 'Whitehead'; indeed he would often heavily pretend that he was the philosopher in person and refer when talking at him to negative prehension and such matters. This was a cause of growing annoyance to John, often expressed by mutterings as he shuffled off down the bar. One Good Friday, a day on which the pubs are of course shut in Dublin, Kavanagh apparently had the luck to meet 'the Pope' O'Mahoney, who was a member of the Zoological Society, and persuaded him to take him up to the Zoo, where drink could be obtained in the members' restaurant. The following day I was in McDaid's.

'I believe Paddy Kavanagh went up to the Zoo yesterday lookin' for drink', remarked a red-faced gurrier who was sitting at the counter.

John looked up from the pulling of a pint and said, 'It's a wonder they didn't keep him there.' Then he paused for a moment, topped off the pint and added viciously: 'I suppose they thought he might frighten the animals.'

The unfortunate Pope was in fact the subject of a classical Irish bull which Kavanagh once made and of which, when I pointed it out to him, he was very proud. We were in the George in Great Portland Street, a B.B.C. pub much frequented by Hibernophiles who worked for the Corporation in various capacities. The Pope was holding forth at great length to an admiring audience while Kavanagh sat and suffered. The performance lasted a long time, but eventually he departed. After he had gone there were murmurs of admiration and appreciation all round. Kavanagh broke in on them. 'That's a terrible bore', he said. 'He must be the greatest bore on God's earth.'

'Oh come now, Paddy', said one of the circle. 'You can't say that. Everyone knows he's a brilliant talker. After all he successfully talks for his dinner'.

'He'd eat a damn sight more if he kept his mouth shut', replied Kavanagh.

I came into McDaid's one Sunday morning to find him

hunched in the seat behind the pillars, the Sunday news-papers strewn around him. I had been reading the *News of the World*, in which a once very distinguished jockey, Tommy Weston, was writing his memoirs.

'I see Tommy Weston is writing his memoirs in the *News of the World*,' I said.

'I see that', said Kavanagh.

'He must be broke', I said.

'Any man at all that's writing anything whatever is broke. Don't you know that by now?' was the Johnsonian answer.

His opinion of most writing was low and it was a rare occasion on which he praised anything. Swift (the 'Verses on the Death of the Dean') William Blake, John Keats and John Clare were the poets who might receive a commenda-tory word or two; while *Moby Dick*, Baron Corvo's *Hadrian the Seventh*, which he never tired of praising, and which he described as one of his bedside books, *Ullysses*, though he had reservations about it; and, for some extraordinary reason Dreiser's *An American Tragedy* and John O'Hara's *Appoint-ment in Samara*, were the only novels I ever heard him mention with approval. He once praised *The Pickwick Papers* in print, but that was only because I had said it had great comic energy and he made it clear that he had not read it. Of his poetic contemporaries only Auden was allowed to have any 'merit' or 'talent', which were his favourite words of commendation. Auden occasionally got high praise, as did Ezra Pound, but this was for Pound's judgments, not for his poems. Others might occasionally be praised if he had met them, but this was usually part of his cultivation of his London myth. Irish poets of course got even shorter shrift than English or American ones. Yeats he 'could do without'. Even dead Irish poets posed some sort of threat to his unique position, and this was particularly the case if they had any pretensions to having emerged from rural Ireland and to share his background. Thus poor Francis Ledwidge was a special target of abuse.

Yet all this was, oddly enough, combined with a great faith in the activity and a sort of collective reverence for the dead who composed the English tradition. The truth was that he did not read very much and when he did it was usually something tried and trusted that he had read before. His contempt for received opinion was extreme and it was partly evidence of his integrity and independence of judgment, partly of his general anarchism and cynicism.

He had no real politics except a sort of anarchism. 'I would blow the whole lot up without scruple or remorse if I could just press a button and no-one would ever know', he once said to me as we walked down Grafton Street, but he had a sort of secondary conservatism which was part of his London myth and his generally Anglophile disposition also. In Irish post-Treaty party politics, about which every Irishman takes sides, he was therefore Fine Gael, or, to put it more exactly, Cumann na nGaedheal. This was part of his pro-British, anti-nationalism.

The Catholic religion, he often said, was 'a beautiful fairy story for children' and it didn't do most people much damage because they didn't really take it seriously, whatever they might think. Sensitive, imaginative people like himself took it seriously, however. In adolescence he had been fool enough to think that everybody did. In reality he was alone in doing so and it did him 'immense damage'.

He had an enormous love for the Irish sub-culture represented by schoolbook poems and ballads and some of the poems in the schoolbooks he had airs to and would sing: 'The Burial of Sir John Moore', 'Lord Ullin's Daughter' and Richard Dalton Williams's 'From A Munster Vale They Brought Her'. He had a perfect ear and was delighted to sing in the right company and on the right occasion. When he had the operation for cancer it damaged his vocal chords somehow and his voice lost its resonance, but his ear of course remained impeccable and he simply adapted his highly individual style to the new possibilities.

5

FORTUNATELY, THIS is not an autobiography. There is no need to tell here of the pains and pleasures of my own life in the years under review, nor, except in so far as they have relevance to the lives of those I am attempting to describe, of my travels and discoveries, departures and returns. Let me here simply say I believe now, looking back, that youth is a disease, for which the only thing to be said is that it is not incurable, and, such are humanity's extraordinary powers of recuperation, leaves few scars. I may as well add while I'm at it that I believe firmly, and as a piece of practical advice, in Christ's injunction about being born again, several times over if necessary. The geographical proximity of this island to its neighbour, as well as the fact that a common language is spoken, provides unattached Irishmen of a literary bent with unique opportunities for various at least partial rebirths, opportunities that I frequently availed of in those years.

But whatever my own fortunes and misfortunes in those years, I do not think that they were happy ones for Brendan Behan. The figure I remember in the two or three years immediately preceding his marriage and his fame was in truth more that of a repetitive performer who had already shot his bolt than that of a brilliant young writer on the verge of a great success. One of his tragedies when success overtook him was to be the knowledge that those who knew him in the days of fame scarcely knew him at all. He was giving only repeat performances, ever more tired, desperate and confused, and needing larger and larger amounts of alcohol to keep them up. The impressarios of the London antics of which the world was now shortly to read had only a dummy figure to manipulate. They benefited from the fact that most of those with whom Brendan came in contact had never seen or heard him before, but they would have done even better had they had the true star that some of us remembered on their hands, bursting at the seams, with his initial sensitivity, his scurrilous comic inventiveness and his peculiar comic grace.

But Brendan was over thirty by the time that anybody paid any real attention to him as anything but a performer, and even then it was as a performer that the larger audience really wanted him. He had therefore a long, too long, experience of the gap that some people feel more acutely than others between their capabilities and their recognised achievement, too long that is for his inner resources. Some people's inner resources are inexhaustible: they go on working away in some hole or corner whether the world wants the product or not. Brendan's inner resources were small, even in the early days. On one of the first occasions he stayed in the wine-cellar he talked of someone who had offered him the loan of a cottage in the Wicklow Mountains. 'But the trouble with this fucking writing', he said, 'is that you have to be by yourself while you're doing it. And that's hard.'

Sometime in the early nineteen-fifties he began to write a twice-weekly column in the *Irish Press*. Since nobody in intellectual Dublin in those days ever saw anything but the *Irish Times*, this was simply not read by most of those he wanted to impress. I was not even aware of it until after he had been at it for more than a year. In fact the very people he cared most for had by then given him up as a bad job.

Brendan carried, therefore, into the broad plains and possibilities of fame, an especially onerous burden: the bitterness of what he felt to be an unwarranted neglect. When fame eventually came to him he was like the Imperial candidate who has waited so long that his dreams of power have turned into dreams of revenge, and who has thought of the prerogatives that will ensure so often and with such intensity that the reality can never provide the expected sensation. When at last he became famous, he had to prove it to himself every day, and others had to repeat continually that it was so. Of course the people from whom such recognitions could never be extracted were those from whom he most wanted them. The possibilities of fame as an instrument of power over others are limited to those who admit its importance, which serious fellow-artists rarely do.

Meanwhile Kavanagh's hostility was implacable and, instead of accepting this, Brendan went about the town creating a sort of intimacy with him by abuse, constantly talking in abusive terms about anybody to third parties being of course one of the best known means of remaining close to them that there is. Now to add to his troubles came the Kavanagh libel action, which, even if it provided him with an obscure and unsatisfactory sort of revenge, reduced his stock still further among the two or three whose respect he most wanted.

Like all Irish countrymen, Kavanagh was highly litigious. He had a great respect for legal forms and phrases and he would often use them in ordinary conversation, accurately or inaccurately, in or out of context. If you taught him a new one, or he picked one up, he would use it for weeks. Worse still, he had the Irish countryman's dream of a bonanza thrown up by an action. In the case of simple folk this takes the form of dreams about damages for personal injury, breach of promise, trespass and whatnot. Kavanagh, being a literary man, dreamed of libel. And, unfortunately for himself, he was libelled. An old-established but attenuated weekly called *The Leader* was rouging its aged cheeks and decided to do a series of sophisticated profiles of contemporary personalities. Among them was Kavanagh.

The piece itself was a typical example of a certain kind of Dublin bad manners, but it was scarcely any more. Dublin is the administrative capital of a small country with a swollen civil service. It is also a University city twice over. Academics and civil servants are frequently of a literary bent, but they are rarely real writers. Dublin therefore contains some hundreds of uncreative literary men, most of them recruited from the provinces and liberated from provincial backgrounds of varying remoteness. To be able to exchange literary gossip, to be 'in' becomes essential for them. The piece complained of was an exercise in a sort of 'innishness' that is highly offensive, but, *sub specie aeternitatis*, not very important.

Unfortunately, besides being litigious by nature, Paddy had a well-sharpened appetite for martyrdom. I understood why in part even then, but I understand better now. There is in every human being a desire for the explainable, clear-cut, black and white circumstance on which we can bring the more obvious emotions about justice and injustice to bear. Paddy was, in a very real sense, the victim of society, but, apart from the suppression of *The Great Hunger* many years before, it was hard to point to any overt act of persecution.

He was largely derided and certainly unsupported, but this, unless in a reasoned indictment of society for its sins of omission, did not amount to a crime against him. His circumstances were almost as bad as were those of many who suffered overt persecution in Russia and elsewhere; indeed, as a consequence, he used to speak with scorn of such writers and their fashionable sympathisers; yet, in his case, there was no actual persecution or dramatic martyrdom to point to. Without perhaps realising it therefore, he decided to bring all his inchoate feelings about this to a head through the medium of a libel action. He decided in fact to achieve martyrdom, and, up to a point, he succeeded brilliantly. By the time he was in the witness box being cross-examined about his character, general reputation and way of life, by the former Prime Minister, John A. Costello, it had been largely forgotten by himself, by his supporters and by the general public that he was the instigator of the action. With a sort of subliminal strategic genius he had succeeded in bringing the whole thing full circle. Like Oscar before him–who of course was also the instigator of the original action–he had become the persecuted one, and before it was over hung high on his cross for all to see, answering his persecutors disdainfully through bleeding lips.

There was one further aspect of the affair, small in itself, which was made to serve the persecution complex brilliantly also. The article was anonymous. This did not seem to me to matter very greatly unless on a personal level, or unless the lawyers could succeed in proving malice, but it was all Paddy needed to link whole segments of the town in a conspiracy against him. It gradually began to be borne in on me that as far as persecution feelings were concerned he was pretty far gone. Aided by whiskey, of which he was now drinking large quantities, and an illness, cancer of the lung, which was as yet undiagnosed, the imaginings of persecution flourished.

For weeks preliminary to the trial one was compelled to engage in speculation as to who had written the offending piece. He would ring me up at *The Bell*, which, bound by some unalterable law of return, I was now editing yet again, and, dropping his voice to the hoarse bellow that passed for conspiratorial tones, begin.

'I say. You know that piece.'

One did of course.

'I've been thinking it over. I was thinking about it all night. I've been putting two and two together.'

There would be a pause here during which one had to make some sound, for he was the most demanding of interlocutors on the telephone, requiring responses even to his silences.

'Do you know what my opinion is, my considered opinion?'

Since he had had several over the last forty-eight hours one could only say something weak like, 'No, what is it?'

'My opinion is that that blackguard so-and-so wrote it.'

This was very likely a name that had already been discussed at length so you could only repeat what you had said the night before. Of course if it was a new name, it was easier to comment; but some of the suggested names were simply beyond discussion.

At length Paddy decided that the piece had been written by (*a*) a University College Dublin historian or (*b*) a well-known civil servant poet or (*c*) both of them together.

But something else suggesting conspiracy was necessary and this was found. The piece was mainly concerned with the *persona* Paddy presented to the world in McDaid's and it had occasional gleams of accuracy as to his line of chat and general demeanour. Therefore a McDaid's informant was postulated. This role was allotted to Behan. Whichever of

97

them had written it, if either of them had written it, or if
it had been written by them both jointly, Behan had been
the 'informer'. Further Behan was being paid by the opposition to follow him round at a distance and spy on him. Why
particularly an informant of 'informer' had been necessary
to help in the concocting of a piece which even the most
amateur of journalists could have managed if its owner had
put his head round the back door of McDaid's for five
minutes, or what such an informer could hope to gain from
cocking his ear to Paddy's conversation in Ryan's or
Mooney's that would be of assistance to anybody in a libel
action in a court of law, was never clear, but such questions
no longer arose. He was now on trial for a nameless offence,
in the realms of literature, philosophy and politics all at
once, in fact, one might say, for mere being, and his enemies
had of course to be credited with employing the traditional
Irish weapons of persecution, including spies and informers.
The objection, if any had the temerity to make it, that
shouting inchoate abuse at a man was a funny way of spying
on him was answered by the theory that Behan was also
employed to upset him and make him do something foolish
which could be brought out in court. The sum which
Behan received was even named: ten shillings a day.

As the time of the hearing came nearer his nervousness
naturally increased, as would anyone's with any temperament whatever. He asked me whether they could 'bring
out' things in his past life against him. I thought this meant
some unnamed foolishness or misdemeanour in his past. It
turned out that to make himself slightly younger he had
been giving the wrong year of birth in biographical notes
for books and the occasional anthology. He had been worry-
ing about this as well as a multiplicity of other things.
Nobody with a highly developed sense of privacy or with
more than the usual number of secrets to guard should ever
engage in legal action. Unfortunately they are the very
people who do.

As a means of raising money the trial was certainly a flop,
since the jury found that there was no libel at all. However,

as an exercise in martyrdom it was, up to a certain point anyway, a superb success. In this respect the other side played
into Paddy's hands by engaging John A. Costello as senior
counsel. Costello was a forceful, occasionally rather savage
lawyer of the old school, dating back to O'Connell, a great
juryman who on this occasion pretended, if that were possible, to be more ignorant of art and letters than the jury
themselves, while concealing behind his pretended baffle-
ment a mind as sharp as a knife. For Paddy's subconscious
purposes he was therefore the ideal instrument and there
took place between them an extraordinary dance of opposites.
One was the poet, high style. The other was the plain citizen
who knew nothing about such matters and was inclined to
be distrustful of them. Costello could not pronounce the
names of certain writers; indeed he affected to find them
somehow funny; and he had never heard of *Moby Dick*.
Paddy, in spite of his alleged peasant cunning and his indubitable desire for the spoils, was a vatic figure who made sometimes obscure but occasionally profound pronouncements
much more suited to the bar of history than the tribunal in
question. Costello kept turning to the jury with a mixture of
sarcasm, condescension to 'the quare poet' and occasional
winks of heavy understanding. Paddy leaned wearily down
from the slopes of Parnassus to deliver his ultimate aesthetic.
It was Mammon and Spirit, Philistine and Poet, even
Marsyas and Apollo.

The purposes of both parties, overt or subconscious, were
further served by a judge who allowed Costello to get away
with what was in effect a plea of justification without actually
introducing one and taking the consequences, that is to say
he allowed him to cross-examine Paddy on the truth of the
article's general picture of his way of life without specifically
pleading that the article was true. There thus emerged a
portrait which was in one light that of a 'character' who
never paid for his own drink: in another that of The Poet
and His Poverty-stricken Way. Both parties were happy
with this. The only difference was that Costello was winning
the verdict of the jury and he knew it, while Paddy was in
all innocence asking for that of posterity.

Unfortunately the tone of the proceedings was somewhat

lowered when he agreed that his work had been praised by Sir Desmond MacCarthy and that he was highly regarded as a Catholic journalist. It did not help either that he should reply when Costello asserted that Austin Clarke was equally highly regarded in the world of poetry: 'He's not in *The Faber Book of Twentieth Century Verse.*'

Yet by and large he maintained his role while Costello gleefully played the heavy straight man opposite him. Histrionically both parties were superb: Costello comically sharing his incomprehension with the jury; Paddy dropping pearls before swine in prolonged, nasal Monaghan vowels which gave an impression of the utmost distaste. Then across this masterly dialectic, subtle and self-contained, fell the outrageous shadow of Brendan. The gods had decided to turn high comedy into low farce.

On the fourth day Costello quietly and without apparent relevance asked him if he was a friend of Brendan Behan's. The object at that stage may only have been to associate him with somebody disreputable. No harm would have been done if Paddy had replied non-committally, or casually, or even declared that he was unfortunately acquainted with the said party. Instead he grew almost hysterical. In high and passionate tones he described Behan as a low blackguard who followed him about, shouting after him in the streets and forcing him to run away. Anybody who knew Paddy and the relationship such as it was could have testified to the truth of this picture. Unfortunately the protest was too shrill. The jury were sharp fellows. They exercised their intelligences in the only way common humanity knows how. They looked for the motive.

When I came out of the packed courtroom Brendan was, oddly enough, in the hallway. He had a heavy growth of beard, the blue suit was even more crumpled and stained than usual and the open-necked shirt was torn down the front. Whatever his role was, that of despised proletarian writer or rough diamond among the dishonest sophisticates, he was got up for it. He was also evidently drunk.

It was a surprise to see him there, for this was the first time he had been anywhere near the proceedings. He shouldered his way through a knot of people towards the outer door and towards where I was standing. I thought he was going to speak to me but he did no more than mutter something about the Monaghan bogman as he passed. I didn't want a scene, but I had hoped for more.

On the next day, early in the proceedings, Costello produced his secret weapon, his Zinoviev letter. Amid the sort of hush which pervades a courtroom when the audience realises that here at last is what it came to witness, he handed Paddy a copy of his own book *Tarry Flynn* and asked him to read the inscription on the flyleaf. It said: 'To my friend Brendan Behan on the day he painted my flat.' The effect was calamitous. The jury now had something they could understand, and they were no longer afraid. Up to that point they had been to some degree intimidated by attitudes they could no more comprehend than they could the mysteries of their own religion, but which a good deal of their conditioning had led them in some obscure way to respect. Now the god had died. Kavanagh was like themselves, a fallible mortal who tried to get away with it when he could. The broad smiles with which they witnessed his discomfiture were those of fellowship and understanding.

The book had of course no relevance whatever to the issues of the trial, but it finished Kavanagh off with the good men and true. What was worse from his own point of view was that it made him uncertain and affected adversely the Parnassian way in which he had hitherto conducted his own part of the proceedings. It was not just that he had been found out, it was that his obsession with Behan and with plots and counter-plots took over. To be too much concerned with anybody, whether through love or hate or fear, or even merely an ungovernable distaste, is to give them power over you.

In fact the moment Costello sprung his trap I had remembered the strange freak of chance that gave him the opportunity. Paddy had been destroyed by the one and only occasion, certainly more than two years before, on which he had ever allowed himself to talk to Brendan in amity. One Sunday night, towards the ultimate end of the Catacombs as a gathering place, there had been a rather nondescript party with a good deal of tuneless song and repetitive argument. At the height of the proceedings, such as they were, in came Brendan, and, to my extreme surprise, Kavanagh. That Kavanagh should have come there was strange enough; that he should have come with Brendan was incredible.

He had a way when entering any gathering of announcing his presence immediately. His was a speaking part, and everybody should know it. Immediately on entering a room or a pub he would deliver himself of his thought of the moment as if it was so exciting that he could wait no longer. On this occasion he came straight over to where I stood and said: 'I've discovered another fallacy. They were telling us lies. It's not true about oil and water. Not true at all. They do mix.' At first I thought he was talking metaphorically about himself and his companion, but it turned out that he meant literally oil and water. The discovery had been made when Behan, who was painting his flat preparatory to the arrival from America of a rich woman in whom he reposed some hopes, had used water instead of turpentine to thin out the paint. How it came about that the same fellow was allowed inside the door I could only guess. In his enthusiasm about the prospect of entertaining the lady, Paddy had evidently assented to the proposition of some third party that Behan was the very man for the job, being in the trade and able to knock off some paint–an important consideration–and Behan of course had leaped at the chance. The day was one of those islands of amity which occur when the stronger, or at least the besieged, party in such a relationship weakens for the moment, nearly always to his subsequent regret. The *rapprochement*, if it can be called such, lasted for that Sunday only, but it was a Sunday which was to rise again above the waters of time, to Kavanagh's amazement and dismay. On that far away day had occurred, all unbeknownst to him, The Convergence of the Twain.

Of course the event served to increase his belief in the prevalence of plots of all descriptions and for the first time–or at least the first time of which I was aware–I fell under suspicion. In the immediate aftermath I suggested that if it was possible, or the lawyers thought it advisable, I should be called to testify to the uniqueness of the occasion on which the book was presented. This was decided against, but not before Paddy has expressed his suspicions to one of the lawyers. 'I don't know who I can trust any longer', he said. 'I'm not even sure if I can trust Cronin.' As it turned out, my father had worked for years for the solicitor in question. 'If he's anything like his father you can trust him with your life', he said, a reply which Paddy had the grace to tell me of immediately.

On the night it all ended he and I and his brother went to the nearby Ormond Hotel. At least four of Paddy's women friends were in and about the place, hoping to be the chosen sympathiser, but we secluded ourselves in an inner room, and there we attempted a statement. When we failed to make much fist of a joint attempt the brother suggested that we should sit down separately, make drafts and then compare and combine them. 'After all, we're all writers here', he said. To which Paddy replied with comic resignation, 'Ay, ay. All brothers of the pen.'

The lawyers countermanded the issue of a statement because an appeal had been decided on. Then the question of costs was discussed between the brothers. Fearing secrets, I attempted to leave, but was told peremptorily to stay. I learned at least a good deal about Paddy's circumstances that I had not known before, including the fact that he was not as badly off as he had led us all to believe. He had at least a proprietory interest in the farm and throughout all the years in Dublin he was in receipt of money from it. Thus, although frequently without cash, he may be regarded as a man with a small private income which, of course, was utterly inadequate to his needs. In the event the question of his having to pay costs never arose. His lawyers appealed; after prolonged argument before the Supreme Court a retrial was ordered; the ancient weekly journal which had published the article was of course utterly unable to sustain further legal action; a small settlement was accordingly arranged; and there the matter died.

There had been no bonanza, but in the aftermath the trial had one important financial consequence for Paddy. When, shortly afterwards, he fell ill, a consortium which included the Archbishop of Dublin, John Charles McQuaid (an old friend), John A. Costello (now Prime Minister again and making generous and gratuitous amends for his role in the proceedings) and Professor Michael Tierney arranged that he should receive an annual stipend for delivering some lectures annually in U.C.D. It was not a princely sum, but it was the long awaited pension and it was to have curious consequences.

In the aftermath of the Kavanagh 'trial' (which of course it was not, but which was how he and I and others now thought of it) I refused to speak to Brendan at all. The handing over of the book seemed to me to have been a particularly shabby and, indeed, a particularly Irish act. It might almost indeed have been part of Kavanagh's scenario for martyrdom, for no matter what he had said about Brendan in the witness box, it savoured of King's evidence. I was a prig of course, indulging myself in a little bit of drama in which I was the haughty incorruptible and Brendan the indubitable villain. I was to pay a penalty. We should beware of the grand gestures which it costs us nothing to make.

Further, I believe now that I was wrong about the facts. He did not give the lawyers the book at all. It was a member of the family in whose house he had left it who, incensed by what Kavanagh had said, handed it over to the defence.

Brendan took the refusal hard. Several times in McDaid's and elsewhere he attempted to speak to me, whether to explain or not I don't know. He was usually drunk and not very coherent, but in any case I would not listen. On one occasion he even embarrassingly went on his knees, begging me to come and have a drink with him. Prig that I was, I refused, and soon the pleadings turned not unnaturally to mutterings, which I ignored also. Finally the mutterings and the occasional bit of abuse flung at me from the middle distance turned to physical assault.

I was sitting by the counter in Davy Byrne's one evening when he came in. He stood a few yards away in the middle of the floor and delivered himself hoarsely of some well thought out if somewhat monotonous remarks about bog-men, kulchies and the like. After a while I had had enough and stood up. What ineffectual form, physical or otherwise, my attempts to shut him up would have taken I do not know, but anyway at that moment the barmen decided, somewhat reluctantly, to do their duty and he was shoohed and persuaded off the premises, though such was their evident nervousness that it became a sort of whistle-stop tour, with Brendan making farewell addresses every few yards of the way.

I stayed till closing time, a matter of a good two hours, and emerged alone. As I came out of the door, adjusting myself to the night, a stertorous being suddenly flung itself out of the darkness, grabbed me by the top of the lapels, behind the neck, and using my own momentum, ran my head forward against the lampost on the edge of the pavement. Even while I saw stars I knew from the 'fuck you' it was Brendan. Hitting a metal lampost with the top of your head at six or seven miles an hour is a trying experience, but fortunately I was not knocked out, and fortunately also Brendan made the mistake of releasing his grip.

What followed was certainly not a fight, but neither, as 'the brides in the bath' murderer is reported to have said, was it fun. I staggered backwards into the middle of the road and Brendan charged after me. Like most dirty fighters he was fond of leading with his head and this was his undoing. I had the old duffle coat that I then wore over my left arm and each time he charged I used it to baffle him. After a while the thing began to become like a bullfight, with Brendan repeatedly rushing and snorting, only to get enveloped every time in the folds of the cape. Luckily for me he had been hanging round for two hours brooding on the wrongs and injustices that were being done to him, so he was by now berserk with rage, while my only thought was self-preservation and I had the icy calmness of fear; but in fact it was his usual insatiable desire for the favour of the generality, that, penetrating even through his rage, turned out his Achilles heel, and saved me in the end.

There had been the normal knot of people in the street at closing time and they were all watching. Brendan had incurred a lot of opprobrium by his initial tactic and now he was being made to look ridiculous as well. Every bull-like rush that he made only to get entangled in the coat was greeted with an ironic cheer and, if the occasional blows that I was able to get in at the top of his head over the coat while I circled away were not very effectual, they were at least crowd-pleasers. When all this began to penetrate to him his dominant passion began to prevail even over his rage, as dominant passions always will, and eventually he rushed no more, but stood still, looked around and delivered himself a few words of abuse to the crowd in general. It was, it seemed, composed of kulchies and bogmen too. It was no use. They were the audience and there was no other and ultimate one before whom they could be made to feel embarrassed or ridiculous. In fact they cheered each remark as they had cheered each rush and so eventually, after standing for a moment in the middle of the road, muttering and evidently at a loss, he gave up and walked away. If to be left in possession of the field was victory, I had it.

A man with an English accent came over and asked me if I was all right. Then he very decently said he was going to Matt Smith's and would I like a lift. I needed a drink and I accepted. We had to walk a bit to his car so when we got out to the bona fide rumours were already circulating which suggested that I had met my end in Duke Street. I was therefore able to fulfil a common ambition by echoing Mark Twain's remark about the rumours of his death being greatly exaggerated, but Kavanagh, who was there with John Ryan, went one better. 'Didn't I tell you the bacon would be no match for the slicer?' he demanded, turning to John.

Next day I found out something about Brendan as a politician. There were at that time two famous Dublin characters who hung about the Duke Street–Grafton Street area pretending to sell newspapers, in fact begging and running occasional small errands for people. As I walked up Grafton Street towards McDaid's that evening one of them accosted me.

'I want to tell yew somethin' about Be'in, Mister Cronin', 'Jimser an' me saw the fight las' night, ef fight ye choose te call it, an' we did'n like what he done to yew at the kick-off. That was a durty trick, Mister Cronin, a very durty trick, an I did'n scruple to tell annywan I was talkin' to today what a durty trick it was. Well Be'in comes up to me an' Jimser after the holy hour an' he asks us to have a drink with

106

em. I did'n mind. I'll have a drink with annywan until he proves his sincerity. So we went into Ryan's with em an' he buys us gargle and buys us gargle until it's comin' out our ears, wherever he got the money.

'Now, I don't want annything from yew, Mister Cronin. I'm ony tellin' ye in case yew heard we was drinkin' with Be'in an' might come to the wrong construction. Of course what Be'in wanted was for me an' Jimser to forget what we seen las' night an' have seen somethin' else entirely. Well, I'll tell ye this much, Mister Cronin. It was too obvious for my taste. Too obvious entirely. An' I don' like the obvious. No I certainly don' like things bein' made too obvious.'

Here, to tell truth, I did the obvious thing myself and offered him one of my last three half-crowns to have a pint. With a pained but kindly look he replied: 'Keep yer money, Mister Cronin. I don't want annything from yew. Yew an' me will have a jar some other day. I'm ony tellin' yew so that yew'll know what a blackguard Be'in is an' that Jimser an' me were ony drinkin' with him for the gargle.'

Of course he was the smartest politician of the three.

Unfortunately, however, the fight, if fight it was, was only the beginning of a prolonged nightmare. Brendan was adept at using the hysteric's weapon and he calculated its many advantages to a nicety. The principal one is that it attracts public attention, from which only the other party suffers, the hysteric having made up his or her mind that he or she is beyond considerations of shame or personal dignity and that so long as the other party retains the capacity to feel either, suffering can be inflicted. Any attempt to reason only brings further indignity with it, for the reasoner is rightly regarded by the bystanders as being somehow hangdog and in need of justification. The striking of women only adds zest to their performance, not to mention bringing other consequences down on the poor consort's head, including the risk of being lynched by the same moralising bystanders. And if the poor fellow actually suffers at the spectacle of the hysteric's own lack of dignity, the victory is complete.

Brendan was neither a woman nor a hysteric, but he constantly used the hysteric's weapon of a public scene from which only one party could be the gainer. If you scarpered, which of course was the sensible thing to do, you would be pursued to the door, if not further, with allegations of cowardice calculated to delight the crowd. On the other hand if you struck him, you would certainly not be the gainer either, for a good messy fight with both parties afterwards barred from the pub—where very likely he was barred already—would bring you right down to his level. You couldn't shout back, for he could outshout Vesuvius. And you most certainly could not reason with him, even if you were talking to him, which I was not.

At the same time his apparent size—when he was in a rage or assumed rage he swelled out, so that he looked enormous; ferocity—all red face and chest—and strength made barmen reluctant to intervene when he pushed open the door of a pub, peered blearily round the interior of the premises, spotted one already cowering in one's corner, advanced with that rolling assertive gait which was perhaps meant to combine the distressed British seaman with a few other *personae*, and began the abuse. I have said shouting, but it would perhaps be wrong to think of him as shouting on these occasions. What he adopted was more the steady, level, hoarse, stentorian tone of the public orator who is intent on drowning out all opposition. Indeed, now that I think of it, drowning out is not a bad metaphor, for the amount of moisture he emitted was considerable and could be felt at a considerable distance.

To make matters worse I was courting a girl. I took her to the pubs I knew because there are advantages to be gained by playing on the home pitch and a bit of capital to be extracted out of the attention you are paid by barmen and even gurrierdom in the places where you are known. At least there should be. In this case the advantages were rather inclined to be outweighed by the omnipresence of Brendan. Besides being beautiful, the girl concerned was literate, and she knew a lot of the people I knew, but all the same she was young, she knew nothing about bohemia and had hitherto heard of McDaid's only by reputation. In this situation the value of the cards that Brendan held was doubled, and he knew it. We would be quietly ensconced in a corner of Davy Byrne's or Neary's when the door would open and with a sinking of the heart I would see the well-known figure poised to roll forward. He would usually stand some yards away, to ensure the maximum of attention from the other people in the pub, and then he would begin. The performance was orotund, more in the style of a labour leader of the old school than of the sharp-witted politicians of today; indeed, passionate as it appeared to be, there was even a touch of leisureliness about it, as if the meeting was scheduled to go on for quite some time. To the girl concerned everything he said was incomprehensible, but the spectacle was frightening all the same; and to me, with my mixture of emotions, the whole thing was agonising. Also, I knew that there was damn-all to be done about it.

I would therefore take her by the hand and flee through the nearest available door. She did not expect, I am glad to say, as other, more orthodox, girls might have done, the prescribed male reactions. Ten or twenty minutes later, in another pub, there would be another performance. Sometimes we were pursued into the alleyway, only Brendan's general lack of locomotion preventing further chase, and as we vanished down a neighbouring street we would hear his voice still grinding and booming away, as one hears the voice of the orator at the public meeting one has left, receding gradually into the distance, until one comes to a place where the traffic noises take over and it is an ordinary summer twilight again.

6

BRIAN O'NOLAN was a small man whose appearance somehow combined elements of the priest, the baby-faced Chicago gangster, the petty bourgeois malt drinker and the Dublin literary gent. The face under the black hat was invariably smooth-shaven, pallid, ageless in a childish but experienced way, thus combining elements of the gangster and the priest. The brim of the hat was wide, as had been fashionable among literary men in Dublin for two generations, but it was bent downwards in front, which added to the baby-faced Nelson effect, as did the generally cross expression of the childishly regular features and small mouth. Besides the hat, which he was seldom without, he almost always wore a dark gaberdine, about which there was something slightly sacerdotal also, even in the way the belt invariably hung down in a loop behind, but which suggested also the clerk or civil servant, garbed for the street and the relaxed converse of the pub.

He had been of course a civil servant to begin with, after what used to be called 'a brilliant career' in University College Dublin, where he was the prodigy of the *avant-garde* littérateurs of his generation. Shortly after leaving there and entering the Civil Service he published a book of amazing virtuosity, *At-Swim-Two-Birds*, which dealt with the novel form in an utterly nihilistic way, while retaining, in dialogue and description, elements of realism far beyond the compass of most novelists. Then with his college reputation and his book behind him, while still in his twenties, he began to write a daily column for the *Irish Times*, which immediately and deservedly attained a local celebrity far surpassing that of any individual piece of journalism that twentieth-century Ireland has known. The book had been published under the pseudonym Flann O'Brien; the column, which was consistently funny, often penetrating and had a cast of characters of its own, was signed Myles na Gopaleen. Of all the remarkable things about it, the standard of hard-edged, incisive prose that its author was able to maintain was perhaps the most so.

It all sounds like a marvellous beginning, but of course it was nothing of the kind. Brian became somehow fixed at a time of brilliant promise and pyrotechnical display, unable to shake off the reputation for prodigious cleverness he had early acquired. This reputation was transplanted from the hothouse confines of U.C.D. to the equally pernicious atmosphere of intimately acquainted Dublin. His humour became the currency of its denizens, the mode of his column their manner of response, to personality, to much in public affairs, even, to some extent, to literature. And by a curious but inevitable inversion he became their creation. He continued to grind out the column, but with the exception of *An Béal Bocht,* a short satirical work in Irish, so far as anybody knew he wrote no more books. 'Myles' supplanted Flann O'Brien, even, in important externals at least, Brian O'Nolan. The latter became known to one and all, even personally, as Myles, and was humoured and tolerated as such. The fate of the licensed jester had befallen him. He existed in and through the response and understanding of his audience.

This ineffably sad process might not have occurred exactly as it did if there had not been flaws in the man himself which made it possible, and of course gigantic public calamities in the world at large which had an effect upon Dublin and on Dublin life, producing exactly the conditions which were needed for it. The creative and personal lives of nearly all the figures in this chronicle were much more deeply affected and distorted by the war than may be immediately apparent. In the case of both Kavanagh and Brian O'Nolan the effect was a curious provincialisation. In both cases, because of the war, Ireland, or, to be much more exact, Dublin, became the sole matrix which formed the developing artist and man. Like all matrices it fitted; it became comfortable and essential. Kavanagh, who was the more individual, and the less nationalistic of the two made more efforts to break out than Myles did. The romantic dream of London, of English fame, of rich women from afar, the deeper and more important yearning for a mode which would fit what he knew to be his ultimate sophistication, the hatred—I mean ordinary hatred here and am not speaking of the plane of being on which that word is creatively transmuted—of things Irish, were all manifestations of a desperate desire to escape entrapment and the slacknesses and wastages of effort which an entrapment in the second-rate produces. That Myles seemed less aware of the necessity is strange, for it was he who suffered most, but then circumstance was against him. Not least was the dazzling early success in a coterie milieu, that of the University. Then there was the transference of this reputation to Myles na Gopaleen and his column, both of which existed again in a coterie context, the coterie in this case being all of vaguely literate Dublin. And for a long time there was the practical circumstance of the job in the civil service, which, though he eventually resigned, or was pressured into resigning from it, had, I think, the effect of narrowing Myles's mind and of making him perhaps too knowing about things which derive their power to corrupt from the fact that all men consider them important. However much the minutiae of the state of the commonweal may have concerned him when he actually had the job, after he lost it a sort of petty spite against officialdom and government caused him to mull over the smaller mistakes and incompetencies of the representatives and servants of the people as if he were some sort of overseer of their efficiency and probity. If he had simply assumed that they were crooks and incompetents and satirised them accordingly, as, for example the urban councillors are satirised in his play *Faustus Kelly,* all would have been well and the purposes of the artist would have been served, but as it was a tone of pained and angry surprise became almost habitual with him. As Kavanagh said one day: 'That kind of stuff would be all right as material for comedy, but the poor fellow actually takes himself seriously as the ratepayers' friend. And that's bourgeois. Worse, it's phony.'

And there were other accidental narrowings and tragedies

Brian O'Nolan (Myles na Gopaleen)

along the way. *At-Swim-Two-Birds* was published on the eve of war. It got one or two good reviews—most noticeably one of Grahame Greene—and it elicited an enthusiastic letter from James Joyce. Then, outside Ireland, it was totally forgotten. It was, as far as reputation and sales were concerned, altogether dead when Longmans' stocks were destroyed by bombing, but of course the physical destruction did not help matters either. It was not until it was reissued in the United States in 1951 that it began to acquire readers outside Dublin and for a long time, even after that, its reputation was word of mouth, not a bad sort of reputation to have, but not necessarily the most gratifying to the author. Something not quite satisfactorily explained as yet happened to the book Myles began immediately after *At-Swim-Two-Birds* and apparently finished early in 1940. This was *The Third Policeman,* an uneven book, said to have been lost and found again. In any case it did not appear until after his death, twenty-five years later. Yet another book, subsequently *The Dalkey Archive,* I myself believe, for reasons which I will come to later, to have been begun and abandoned about this time. His play, *Faustus Kelly,* which certainly deserved better of a Dublin audience, flopped at the Abbey in 1943. All in all, as far as the circumstances of publication and reception are concerned—and let nobody who has not had to struggle with them sneer at their importance—it was not a happy literary history. Yet, through all poor Flann O'Brien's tribulations, Myles na Gopaleen continued to be one of the most celebrated of Dubliners and his column, unfailingly brilliant and brilliantly adjusted to its Dublin audience, continued to appear daily.

That Myles had an abundance of comic material at his disposal is evident; and yet after the early starts and false starts, he largely failed to get his Dublin into books; so that there is certainly truth in the remark Kavanagh made one day to the effect that 'poor Myles'—his usual locution—'has utterly failed to find a myth that would carry all that stuff in his column, that would lift it into art.' It was a question of finding a fictive or imaginative structure, and perhaps, after all, the nihilistic structure of *At-Swim-Two-Birds* had been too brilliant.

The column gave pleasure to a great many people and occasionally perhaps the authentic delight to a few, but it must have been a terrible burden, and as ruinous in the long run as the drink. The penalty of journalism, and kindred activites, is that it gives its author a certain amount of warranted creative satisfaction. Having done a nice, neat, expert job with a good joke or two in it, you are inclined to turn on your heel and walk away feeling pleased with yourself, and of course entitled to leave it at that for the rest of the day. I am not speaking contemptuously of journalism now; indeed a writer who has practised it hardly ever does. He enjoys it in fact, perhaps too much, and he can hardly ever bring himself to do a sloppy job, knowing too well that those who inure themselves to doing sloppy jobs sooner or later become incapable of doing anything else, in any medium.

Myles was proud of his column, as who that could do it would not be? He would often rehearse a joke that was to appear a few days later and he was always pleased if you adverted to something that had been in it, but it must have torn his guts out over the years. The fact that it was humorous in intent and that he could and did adopt any one of a multitude of ironic levels, saved him to some extent from becoming the cantankerous preacher, the corrector and arranger, but it was a temptation to him nonetheless, particularly in the later, more embittered years. When I knew him first I used occasionally be driven to fill up the pages of *The Bell* with portentous rubbish which, I am afraid, at the time I took all too seriously. I had failed to develop any ironic devices or protections of my own and the tone of voice was all wrong. One day he spoke about these articles. 'You know what you're in danger of becoming?' he said. 'You're in danger of becoming the public-house orator, who knows he's in the right and is determined to enjoy it.' It was an acute comment, which I never forgot, but I thought then and have thought since that the fact that he made it proved that he knew something about the dangers himself.

In the early fifties the column appeared about three times a week. It was written, as far as one could judge, in the very early morning. Then he came into town with the copy and drank through the forenoon and early afternoon. Like many thoroughgoing alcoholics he had an early bedtime and because of sleeplessness and morning thoughts and the jigs in general a very early rising. He was no stranger to the markets pubs, which open at seven o'clock, and in which there is a certain freemasonry among the wide assortment of characters who are driven from their beds by mental and physical distress in the early morning; indeed many of his jokes had them as location. I remember discovering some months after there had been a revision in the licensing laws in Dublin that Myles was ignorant of the new evening closing time, which of course was a primary preoccupation with everyone else, but he knew what time they opened in the morning all right. He was, I think, a true alcoholic, which is more than I think Behan was, or Kavanagh either. Of course the disease, if it is there at all, becomes more pernicious as one grows older, but I think what happened in Behan's case was that he deliberately made drink so much a part of his *persona* that he could never thereafter separate himself from it for fear that the act would collapse. I remember one morning in Cusack's in the early days when he and I were first up and came down to the kitchen to find an open bottle of gin, left over from our revels of the night before, standing on the table. We both felt like a drink, but there was nothing to put in it and neither of us would touch it as it was. When Ralph came down to find us still staring at our separate measures of gin and water he remarked drily that whatever else we made, we would never make Grade A alcoholics. Of course Behan was later on a diabetic and that made an enormous difference, not only to his tolerance, but to how he probably felt in the mornings, so that his apparent need for a curer must have been, in later years, extreme. And of course also there is a certain point where the toxin in the system takes over and does the rest, creating its own need, so that there is no escape from the cycle of ghastliness and temporary recovery. Kavanagh began to drink whiskey in the dark days, round about 1953, because he was sick to death of the struggle; and I think he was polishing it towards the end because he knew that he was creatively finished. In one of the last conversations—I mean real conversations—

we had he said he had 'no lumber in his mind'. 'That fellow Auden', he said, 'has a well-stocked mind. He has a lot of furniture, a lot of philosophy and psychology and that sort of thing. Of course it's junk, but it does to make a blaze, it creates energy and a sort of warmth, and when you get the blaze going you might succeed in saying something. But I've read nothing and have no rubbish to burn. None at all, no philosophy, no nothing. And you can't go on writing lyrics.' In fact the *Collected Poems* do give the impression of a man who was, happily enough, finished. He had written his poems of celebration and then he had written some celebrating the writing of them. And that was that. In his case too, the toxin probably took over and demanded its own price, but his drinking, in its complete abandon and absence of remorse, has always seemed to me to have been more deliberately suicidal than anybody else's I have known.

Be that as it may, Myles, I am convinced, was a true alcoholic, with a built-in physiological need for alcohol. Signs on, he was a sober drinker, meticulous and methodical. He seldom drank anything but Irish whiskey, which he watered to taste and placed to his elbow like a serious man. He was inclined to be cantankerous, but he had no interest in fun and games. Drink and the monologue which was his idea of conversation sufficed him. In temperament he was *petit bourgeois*. Dressed always in collar and tie, raincoat and hat, he was very scrupulous about the buying of his round and disapproved of those who did not or could not support themselves. He referred to Kavanagh frequently as 'the Monaghan toucher'. Of course it was easy for Myles to talk, since on leaving the civil service he had been allowed his pension, but in all things he was the reverse of bohemian, a quiet little man who liked good service in old-fashioned pubs, was respectably married and had his own home in the suburbs. The thought of sexual promiscuity was abhorrent to him; indeed, it may be, the very thought of sex itself. I used occasionally bring my girl, who was in truth as fair and fresh an example of Irish femininity as you could find, to McDaid's at lunchtime, and one day he referred to her as 'Cronin's huer'. All breaches of the conventions or disturbances of order were likely to annoy him. One afternoon a friend and I went to immense trouble to leave him home. We had been out to the Strawberry Beds, which he believed was the widow Flavin's, and into which he would not go, so that whiskeys had to be ferried out to the car for him. When eventually he decided to be taken home he insisted several times that we were going in the wrong direction and taking him somewhere else entirely for our own nefarious purposes. When we got to the house we waited until he was safely in and then my friend began to turn the car in the roadway. During the course of this there was a minimal collision with another car which was coming up. The driver of the other car made a big fuss; the police had to be fetched from Donnybrook police station and the road measured, the whole thing taking perhaps three-quarters of an hour.

Suddenly Myles appeared again at his hall-door. He was now wearing a pair of striped pyjamas, but he had his hat and raincoat on as usual. He stood for a moment sternly eyeing the scene. Then he delivered his condemnation. 'Would yes get those motor cars out of there immediately and not be blockin' this thoroughfare?' he demanded. 'There's decent respectable people live here in this road that pay their rates and taxes and have a right of unimpeded passage up and down it. And they don't want any criminals or chancers round here that are an object of interest and concern to the police force.'

Sometimes, of course, drink being what it is, his generally respectable demeanour and get-up would be discomposed. One day while I was sitting with him at the counter in McDaid's he had a sneezing fit. When it was over some mucus remained on his tie and shirt front. Kavanagh, who was sitting further up, commented gratuitously and audibly more than once on what he chose to call 'the disgusting state' he was in. It penetrated to Myles that the references were to himself, so he naturally took umbrage, and, snarling about 'the Monaghan toucher', he left his stool and attempted an assault. There was something terrier-like about Myles and when he was angry he yielded to no man. Kavanagh retreated, tittering at first and pretending that the attack was a comic matter. Then he suddenly got terrified and dashed behind the counter. I got Myles back to his seat, but it was some time before Kavanagh, now talking loudly to all who would listen about blackguardism and violence, could be persuaded to come out.

Throughout 1953 and 1954, the year of the Kavanagh libel action and the Behan imbroglio, there were very few people in McDaid's, day or night. All the pubs were doing badly and, for a number of reasons, McDaid's was particularly deserted. By some law of compensation, the lunchtime habitués, though small in number, were particularly distinguished, I suppose because literary men, being poor to begin with, will continue to drink on whatever the general state of the economy. But even though there might be only three or four people in the pub, as a general rule Myles preferred not to be with Kavanagh. He had certainly some respect for the poet, but he rather disliked the man. Kavanagh's attitude was ambiguous. He often quoted the column and found much to amuse him there, and he would say, for instance, 'that little na Gopaleen is the only man of sophistication in the whole bloody country', but in the next breath he would be speaking pityingly of 'poor Myles's' failure.

He affected to believe that the play *Faustus Kelly* was the best thing Myles had ever written and often adverted to 'the great laugh' he had 'got out of it', but this of course may have been a way of denigrating *At-Swim-Two-Birds,* for even a prose writer, and particularly an *avant-garde* anti-novelist like Myles, could pose a threat to the ghostly eminence he claimed.

Some time in, I think, 1954 Myles asked me to come up to the Painter Sean O'Sullivan's studio with him during the holy hour 'for a chat'. It was possible at that time to obtain poteen which was brought up from the west of Ireland by a man who made a weekly journey on behalf of the Board of Works. Somewhat to my surprise Myles bought a bottle of this.

O'Sullivan's studio was in a house in Stephen's Green, otherwise given over to offices, and when we got there we found that he was not in and that the place was locked, so we sat on the stairs outside his door, drinking the poteen, which was excellent stuff, out of the neck of the bottle, while the occasional typist tripped up or down past us. He told me many things about himself and he discussed his creative difficulties. It was fifteen years since *At-Swim-Two-Birds* had appeared and with the exception of *An Béal Bocht* and the play *Faustus Kelly,* there had been nothing in between. He spoke of going away somewhere, 'to Mount Melleray or Tory Island', to write a novel he had in mind, which would be 'a study in the banal.' I was dubious about the idea of the monastery or the island, which struck me as romantic notions, not at all suitable for a city-dweller of his temperament. He said it was essential to get off the drink and he didn't see how it could be done otherwise. I said I didn't think the drink mattered all that much, though he would be as well off to give it up if he could, but I did urge him to suspend the column for a while if he could manage without it. However, he was struck on the idea of some sort of penitential retreat or incarceration and he said that he had discussed the matter with O'Sullivan who had agreed to come with him. This seemed to me to put the proposal in an even more dubious light, for if there was one man in Dublin who was fonder of drink than himself it was the same Sean.

However, he was so enamoured of the idea that it seemed best to keep him going. If the thought of another book had become entwined in his mind with the image of a bare and Spartan place, why not? Accordingly, to encourage him I pointed out that if he could average six hundred words a day he would have his book finished in a little over three months. Immediately he rounded on me.

'Is it six hundred words a day? Six hundred? Sure them Victorian fuckers wrote six thousand words every day before breakfast,' he declared. I had touched him on the quick, his journalist's pride in his capacity.

While he sat there on the steps also he talked about life and told me a story about a man who had found occasion to complain to his wife about the state his shoes were in, 'What sort of a woman are you at all?' he had asked her, 'that you couldn't even polish a man's shoes?'

To which she had replied: 'I'd polish them all right if you ever took them off, but since you go to bed every night with them on I don't have much chance.'

This story seemed to have some sort of symbolic significance for him and to amuse him greatly. He laughed his rather high-pitched little laugh till the tears came. Then he reminisced. 'Lots of women wanted to marry me', he said, 'because they thought they were going to get taken to the Royal Hibernian Academy and first nights at the Abbey and all that sort of cultural stuff. Little they knew. The only time I was ever at a first night in the Abbey was the first night of *Faustus Kelly*, and that was a disaster.'

The book to which he was referring that day may have been *The Hard Life, An Anatomy of Squalor*, a short novel which finally appeared some years later while I was in Spain, but as we shall see, it could have been *The Dalkey Archive*, which I believe may have been begun many years before and left uncompleted, to his and its detriment. *The Hard Life* is not a very considerable work, but it has considerable virtues. It is funny all through and it has one or two really hilarious scenes. Within its limits it is very nearly flawless and it succeeds in communicating a vision. It could have been written by the author of *At-Swim-Two Birds*; and though it is obvious that its author is limiting his ambitions, it is not necessary to explain any falling off in his powers. The same, alas, cannot be said for *The Dalkey Archive*, which appeared in 1965, shortly before his death, but of that more later.

Many of the events I have been chronicling took place in the year 1954. What with the empty pubs and the ferocious discordances within them there was a certain atmosphere of gloom and rancour about. And for some of those in this chronicle it certainly was not a happy time. Kavanagh had pinned his hopes of fortune on the libel action and had been sorely disappointed. He took some consolation from what nowadays would be called the coverage it got. For day after day there was a two page spread in the *Irish Times*. Costello, whatever else he had done, had certainly succeeded by his cross-examination and the responses it elicited in adding to the Kavanagh legend. People who had never read a line of poetry; who were not sufficiently in the Dublin swim to have heard the Kavanagh jokes and the Kavanagh stories; who did not frequent his pubs; were now aware that they had a poet in their midst. 'I'm as famous as De Valera', he said one day. And then he changed his mind and pitched it higher. 'No. I'm as famous as Martin Moloney,' he declared, naming the wonder jockey of the era. And though he might have intended through his answers and statements to give another picture of the poet, the one that had emerged was oddly like the stereotype the race had cherished since the days of Eoghan Ruadh: the poet was wild, indigent, gregarious, verbally fluent and over-fond of a drop. Since we were shortly to enter a time when good people in the suburbs and elsewhere who cared nothing for poetry and had no intention of troubling themselves with it were yet to feel, and to be encouraged to feel, that they should know something at least about it, even if only on a personality level, Kavanagh had a head start. When that day dawned, as it was just about to, he would be 'the poet'. Thus, in a sense, one of his ambitions was achieved. The shadowy laureateship was his.

But whatever remote satisfaction he might have derived from this outcome, there were other factors which did not add to his hopes or his cheer or his temper. The possibility of having to pay costs was to hang over him until the Supreme Court finished its deliberations. He was now well and truly polishing the whiskey. He had come more or less to the end of one creative burst, the *Kitty Stobling* poems, and it was to be some time before he would be able for another. Above all, he was suffering from an undiagnosed ailment, cancer of the lung, for which he would have to undergo an operation the following year.

It is possible that these factors account for certain duplicities in his attitudes to his friends which had become apparent to me, chiefly through the tale-bearings of a third party. They had not yet reached the stage of paranoiac symptoms, though I think it is fair to say they did towards the end. A recent collection of some part of his letters, privately published somewhere in America, give an impression of him, I believe, as an unscrupulous hypocrite all the way along the line. However, it is perhaps better to be charitable and to believe that in the earlier days at least his own attitudes and declarations meant something. The worst that can be said, I believe, is that until towards the end when he was really tortured by dark suspicions and delusions, he played sometimes a double game with certain gullible people, either in the hope of pleasing them by giving them an extra taste of sole intimacy, or simply on the principle of divide and rule. Some of these people were indeed gullible enough, and since he encouraged more than one of them to feel that they were his sole confidant, in fact encouraged what almost amounted to a sort of possessiveness, he had, among the more weak-minded anyway, fertile ground for creating the sort of illusion his perhaps understandable mendacity of nature thought to be an advantage to him.

Whatever about Kavanagh's general state, in Behan's case, towards the end of the year anyway, appearances may have been deceptive. To the outside observer, who saw him, as I now saw him, only at a distance and in public houses he appeared almost a write-off, though in fact his creative period, such as it was, had just begun or was just about to begin. He must have been writing *The Quare Fellow* about this time, for it was produced towards the end of the year, but writing is done in private, while other things, alas, are done in public, the more spectacular kind of drinking being one of them.

Looking back, in fact, on 1954, it seems to me now that secrecy was the order of the day and that anything that was being done at all was being kept under wraps, for fear of somebody else finding out. There was too much jealousy and betrayal about for things to be otherwise—too much hunger as an acquaintance of mine used to say.

It was therefore nothing out of the ordinary when John Ryan came into Davy Byrne's and said there was something he wanted to tell me about, but that it would be necessary to pledge me to secrecy in advance. I assented, silently, over an invisible pint of stout, and was told about a small celebration he and Myles na Gopaleen had planned for June 16th in which only a very limited number of people–the two organisers, Patrick Kavanagh, Dr A. J. Leventhal, a dentist by the name of Joyce who was a distant relative of the novelist and myself were to be allowed to take part. June 16th was of course Bloomsday, though that was a word not much used then; and June 16th 1954 would be the fiftieth anniversary of the day on which Joyce's great fiction about a Jewish Irishman of dubious morals and in many ways unprepossessing aspect was supposed to take place in Dublin. Our celebration would be the first.

In terms of the general atmosphere of the time it was no surprise either when a day or two later Brian O'Nolan, otherwise Brian Ó Nualláin, alias Myles na Gopaleen, alias Flann O'Brien, came into another establishment and declared that he had a small proposition to put to me but that it would be necessary to go somewhere else before the exact nature of it could be unfolded for there were too many dangerous people–chancers and intriguers and go-betweens and Johnny-come-latelys of all descriptions–in the pub we were in.

We went elsewhere, but Myles was not in fact so far gone in secrecy that he refrained from telling me what he was talking about. I gathered that it was something he had decided to call 'the jant', which was to take place when you know, the day of your man's book. He hoped I would come on 'the jant' but I was to tell nobody else whatever about it, and I was to particularly refrain from telling our mutual friend Con Leventhal that he would be symbolically representing the Jewish community on the day in question.

Well, the day of the jaunt came round. We were to assemble at Michael Scott's house, beside the Martello tower, and in two horse-cabs retrace the route of the funeral procession and Stephen's morning itinerary. I travelled out with Kavanagh and John Ryan. The horse-cabs were there, horse's noses deep in the bags. Early in the morning though it was, Myles appeared to be deep in something else; while Paddy, even on the journey out, appeared to have been absorbing refreshment by some secret chemical process known only to himself. To get to the tower from Michael Scott's garden in those days it appeared to be necessary to climb a small sloping rock face and cross a barbed wire fence. Myles decided to embark on the climb and Kavanagh, not to be outdone, elected to do the same, and proved as might be expected the better climber. The thing was not much more than twelve or fourteen feet high and was by no means sheer, but it presented certain difficulties to the two climbers just the same, and as they started up the little cliff a serious altercation began. Kavanagh, perhaps out of fear, went faster than before, so fast indeed that his feet were soon about the level of Myles's head, which meant that he was about the height of a smallish man above the ground, for Myles had not succeeded in ascending very far.

When Myles was drunk and angry he snarled, and he was snarling now. Suddenly he grabbed at Kavanagh's ankle and attempted to pull him down. Though the fall which could have resulted might not have been the cause of serious injury there was also the possibility that Kavanagh, now nervously shouting for help and beginning to slip, would, intentionally, in panic, or by accident kick him in the face, and a kick from Kavanagh, who had such enormous feet that he had to have his boots specially handmade, would be like a kick from a trip-hammer. All parties therefore rushed to the rock to restrain Myles who, however, in typical terrier fashion, refused to give up his grip on his victim's ankle. Finally his hand was prised loose, but the doing of this was not made easier by Kavanagh's violent thrashing movements with the imprisoned foot; and I must confess that, as I assisted in the operation, I was highly fearful that I might get the aforementioned disastrous kick in the face myself.

This little contretemps over, we boarded the two horse-cabs that Myles had provided for and set off at a good jog trot along the route. Two things transpired during the course of the day which would have pleased Joyce. First, the dentist turned out to have a tenor voice which is endemic in the family, and he knew and consented to sing the master's favourite song, 'Silent, O Moyle, Be The Roar Of Thy Waters'. I am not sure that the singing pleased Myles, who sat silent and apparently disapproving during it. I think in fact he would have preferred us to proceed respectably, preserving an Edwardian decorum, like the bourgeois who followed the funeral in the horse-cab in the book, whom, in his old-fashioned way, he somewhat resembled. Although a tacit reconciliation had been effected, he seemed to blame Kavanagh and muttered at intervals about him.

The other matter was the result of the Ascot Gold Cup. June 16th 1954 was not only the fiftieth anniversary of the day Joyce had picked on as the day of his great fiction, but it was also one of the comparatively rare occasions when the date coincides with the Thursday of Ascot week and the running of the Ascot Gold Cup, as it does in the book. Naturally, with Kavanagh, Con Leventhal–also a racing man–and myself in the party, some attention was given to this. Our progress, what with stops at pubs and places of interest such as Sandymount Strand, was so slow that the race was actually run while we were still in transit, in fact while we were still traversing the route of the funeral; and, at the insistence of the racing men, we stopped at a book-maker's in Irishtown to have a bet and hear the broadcast. There was a very strong French favourite, owned by M. Marcel Boussac, reputedly a great stayer. As is often thought advisable in the Gold Cup, the stayer had a running mate who was meant to act as pace-maker and ensure a good gallop for him, so that the stamina limitations of the other horses in the race would be exposed. The pace-maker's name was Elpenor and he proceeded to make the running to such effect that not even his own stable-companion, who was supposed to win, could catch him, and he perforce went on to win the race himself at fifty to one, a record price for a Gold Cup winner in this century, though Throwaway in the book starts at forty to one.

Now Elpenor is a character in the *Odyssey*. He is a com-panion of Ulysses who falls off a height during some fighting, as some of our party had so nearly done, cracks his skull and dies. Although Ulysses remarks that it didn't much matter, 'since he wasn't much of a fighting man, nor ever very strong in the head', he nevertheless goes down into the underworld after him to see what he can do. This descent is paralleled in the book by the scene in Glasnevin cemetery, for in Joyce's *Ulysses*, Elpenor is represented by the deceased Paddy Dignam; and it was the route of Paddy Dignam's funeral that we were following; indeed the whole idea of a commemoration which would involve horse-cabs grew out of the Dignam funeral sequence.

Needless to say, when I explained all this to Kavanagh—and it was necessary to explain some of it—he accused me of withholding information. What makes the result the more remarkable was that Joyce always believed his book to have strange prophetic powers of which he himself only became aware after the event. Suffice it to say that before the event none of the commemorative party spotted the tip, not even A. J. Leventhal, a learned man in several languages and Registrar of Trinity.

The trip, I am glad to say, ended happily in the back bar of the Old Bailey. The jealousies among the mountaineers of the morning seemed to have been forgotten and relations between Myles and Paddy were as good as I ever remember them to have been.

Towards the close of the year Peadar O'Donnell passed on the word to me that through the good offices of the Irish-Soviet friendship society, the Society for Cultural Relations with Foreign Countries in Russia (VOKS) would be glad to entertain a group of Irish writers and artists and to show them something of the Soviet Union. Would I take charge of the composition of the party, which was to leave in January? The prospect seemed to me to hold limitless possibilities and I immediately set about organising a party which would give the Russians something to think about as well as being amusing in and for itself.

Among others I asked both Myles and Paddy and both immediately accepted. Then the whole thing began to be like the parable of the wedding guests. One by one, those I had asked began to find reasons for not going. Kavanagh thought a trip to the Soviet Union would prejudice the success of his appeal against the verdict in the libel case. Myles said that his mother was not well and in the circumstances he would not like to be so far away from Ireland. The party that eventually did go was very different from that I had originally hoped for, which was a pity. The trip was an eventful one, but the events were rather different from those that might have taken place had Paddy and Myles been present.

I have one further memory of 1954, and that is again of a Christmas day. My girl friend, who had a flat in Adelaide

Road, was going home for Christmas and, bearing in mind that it was the season of goodwill I invited Kavanagh round to the flat, which was cosy enough when the fire was lit. I had got a bottle of whiskey on credit in McDaid's and bought some steak and potatoes which I cooked. It was not exactly Christmas fare, but I allowed it would be better than the stale herring he would have said was all he had at home. At first he would not eat, complaining that he was not well. Then he polished off a good half-pound of steak and a plateful of mashed potatoes and congratulated himself on 'being able to get that wee snack down'. We drank the whiskey and while we drank I played an old John MacCormack record of 'Bantry Bay'. He asked me to play it again and then again, until finally we must have played it at least a hundred times. Whenever I hear it now it reminds me of that Christmas.

It was a happy enough day, after a fashion. After we had finished the whiskey we made some urgent phone calls and finally John Ryan came round with another bottle and some turkey and ham, so in the end we had our Christmas fare.

In the spring of the year Paddy had been surprised that I did not appear to be going on my annual migration to London. I did not tell him the reason for a while, but when he met her he appeared to be full of approval. She and he became friends and managed to remain so even through the erraticisms of the very end.

When I came back from Russia in February of the next year we got married. We hadn't asked anybody except a few relatives to the ceremony, which was performed in Haddington Road Church, but Paddy turned up. He also came with us to Tommy Ryan's pub afterwards and, subsequently, to lunch in the Dolphin. He remarked that you never met anybody's relatives except at weddings and funerals, and that, anyway, up to this point he had thought I was like Jesus Christ, who did not produce his brethren in public.

Three days before ours, an item concerning Brendan Behan's wedding appeared in the papers. He, too, had kept it pretty dark.

7

SOHO WAS largely inhabited by failures, the ruined men of the forties, whom the war had somehow confirmed in a natural dislike for the mere struggle for circumstantial success. If the whole structure is being blown up around you the name of the game is apt to change. In North Soho, during the war years, a true bohemia had flourished and, in a measure, a true anarchy prevailed. The sort of artist who emerged from it was apt to be a higher type than the success-oriented younger poets or painters of the fifties, but he was also apt to be a more than usually highly developed misfit. Even where big-time circumstantial success came to one of the war babies, as, for example, it did to Dylan Thomas, there was likely to be a pretty highly developed *nostalgie de la boue* in his attitude towards it. There were old Soho hands who were still about to be overtaken by the success machine, such as Francis Bacon, but in his case, as in others, overtaken is almost literally the word, and the success would be the result of a defiance of the world and its fashions rather than a cultivation of them. And there were others whom success had passed by or who had simply lost whatever interest they had had in it.

None of these people made a virtue or a life-style out of rejection or bohemianism, as, very shortly, another generation were to do, and as do the hangers-on, the amateurs and the free-loaders in any such *milieu*. They knew that artists as well as many other people had been poor and that some people must accept poverty as preferable to the waste of time and the corruptions inherent in the struggle to avoid it. They were aware also that though the conditions of living and the production of works of art are to some extent intertwined, it is the uncreative who are most likely to confuse a mere lifestyle with a creative discovery.

Soho itself, to most people who drank there, was then a pleasant backwater and a geographical convenience, a place where there were several pubs within a short stroll of each other, where the drinking clubs were entitled to remain open in the afternoon and where fellow-spirits of some sort as well as one's friends could be found. There was also the general preferability of the indigenous inhabitants of the area to the ordinary English; the fact that it had a built-in tolerance to eccentrics of all descriptions, artists as well as criminals; and that a backdrop of delicatessens, off-licences, small shops and restaurants was preferable to many other settings. It was, too, a village, and therefore satisfied something in the soul that abhorred metropolis. On a fine day once could stand at a corner or take a turn in the sunlight through fairly still and uncrowded streets. In those days there were really only the restaurants and the delicatessens to attract the outside world. The street-walkers were still there, but they were a homely enough lot, settled in years and, probably, in custom, and the multitudinous strip clubs were not to begin to appear until the end of the decade. When they did, Soho accepted them as it did everything else; they are now so omnipresent as to have largely changed the look and the ambience of the area; but in any case the afternoon drinking clubs, devoted to drink and drink only, which were to many the primary facility that Soho had to offer, have been swept away.

I first went to Soho because what little acquaintance I had in London seemed to drink there; in the very first instance, I think, to meet Lucien Freud, whom I had known in Dublin. In my earlier sojourns in London it had become to some extent the home from home, the ghetto that Irishmen seek, but even there I was lonely through lack of acquaintance until one summer day when I was standing by myself at the bar of the old Caves de France, Robert MacBryde, whom I knew to see, came over to me and said, of all things for a lonely man to hear, 'Ye have a nice face. I'd like to meet you. My name is Robert MacBryde', and held out his hand. He was with Robert Colquhoun and

130

Paul Potts and one or two others. He was about to return to Scotland for the first time in many years, to open an exhibition in Edinburgh, and he had quite a lot of money with him, given to him apparently by the Arts Council for the trip, out of which he was paying his debts in the bars. At this time the Roberts lived in Essex, in an old mill-house which they shared with Elizabeth Smart and her children; and their visits to Soho, like those of other country dwellers such as Dylan Thomas or George Barker, were in their circle something of an event.

Like, I think, everybody else, I sensed their quality immediately. They had that curious directness of the Scots, which is so attractive to an Irishman, accustomed to charm but suspicious of what it conceals. In Colquhoun there was very nearly no concealment at all, or only as much as makes life possible for any human being, and particularly a very shy man. If there was any concealment in MacBryde, it was often a product of good manners, and only later of circumstance. Embellishment is another thing and so is reserve; MacBryde was certainly an embellisher and Colquhoun was reserved. The appearance of both was an extraordinarily accurate index to character, and they made a strangely contrasting pair. Colquhoun was tall, roughly handsome, every feature open and strongly marked, the sort of long head that one associates with the Scots who have gone around the world as makers, builders and engineers. He was somewhat awkward and most inarticulate, but his gentleness and warmth came across immediately because when you met him you met almost the whole man. MacBryde on the other hand was small, and constantly in deft movement, even the way he picked up a glass or handled a cigarette suggesting precision and sensitivity to nuance and detail. He had a round head with the prominent, bushy eyebrows and the mobile rubber features of the clown, or perhaps of some sophisticated, disillusioned, rather tired French cabaret artist. He was as quick on the uptake as he was in movement. I have heard people speak of his malice, but I never experienced it, except in the case of people who had pushed him beyond bearing, and he certainly had a gift of intimacy, so that whatever he might have said he restored confidence and the flow of feeling immediately when you met him again. He was remarkably talented in every way. He sang and danced in modes all his own and he was a first-class cook. His feeling for the physical reached out to embrace the most trivial things, from buttons to boot polish, and he could improvise almost anything in almost any circumstance. I remember him ironing with a heated tablespoon and boiling handkerchiefs in salt.

As appearance was an accurate indication of character, so was character of their paintings. MacBryde's feeling for what he called the *matière,* for the handling and application of paint, was intense and delicate. Somewhere far back, probably at the Glasgow School of Art, he had discovered Braque and had been dazzled, but characteristically by the superb, perhaps even over-smooth, technique rather than by any profundity in the analysis of objects. He had taken Braque and lightened him, substituting for the master's dark harmonies of colour and design more overtly decorative patterns, retaining the humble objects and the interest in disposing them to best effect. Like his master, MacBryde was a pure painter, with nothing very profound to say. The difference perhaps between superb talent, such as Robert had, and great genius like Braque's, is that the latter can survive that condition, making indeed a rewarding state in itself out of the absence of 'something to say', whereas when MacBryde's decorative impulse failed him he had nothing left.

By contrast, Colquhoun was almost literary, giving the impression of having a great deal of something or other to say, though not always of being certain of his means as a painter. If MacBryde had early taken Braque and lightened him, Colquhoun had taken Picasso, and made of him a more monumental, hieratic painter even than he is. It was the Picasso of the thirties, of those suffering, solitary, disassociated faces that originally attracted him, and his own figures and animals are marooned in a solitude redeemed only by an indestructible grandeur, particularly strong in the case of his old women. The technique is cubist, the figures largely made up of primary forms, but it is used for expressionist rather than naturalistic purposes, each figure

132

unnaturally stiff and disposed for eternity. Both people and animals are thus figures of portent and they are somewhat burdened by this portentousness. It is possible that in this sense Colquhoun had too much to say and was finally almost overwhelmed by the difficulty of his vision.

MacBryde, in drink and out of it, sometimes abusively, sometimes otherwise, was later to speak of their first acquaintance, of Colquhoun's Presbyterian—according to him—puritanism and to allege that it had taken him a long time to break down the puritanical barriers. It may have been so. Whether there was not more to it than that and whether he ever succeeded is another matter. Part of the whole story I was not to learn until they were both dead and I had better reserve what I learned for its place. Suffice it to say here that MacBryde was in any case a natural, though fastidious, enjoyer, a bon vivant in the true sense. He must early have got rid of his own inhibitions and he must certainly have had many to contend with in Colquhoun's case. As we all know, the removal of inhibitions can be a dangerous process, and it is possible that he destroyed other things as well.

They must, though, have made a marvellous and marvellously attractive pair in those far-off days. The Scots working class, from which MacBryde came, rank high in the human scale and in the town of Maybole in Ayrshire they did not have to contend with the degrading conditions of the city slums, but it must none the less have been a strange eventuality that produced the young Robert. Colquhoun's people, from nearby Kilmarnock, were a step higher in the financial scheme of things, being craftsmen and artisans, engineers and draughtsmen and so it was an environment more likely to produce a painter. They met at the Glasgow School of Art, both of them still in their teens, experimenting with this and that, MacBryde doubtless the more sophisticated of the two: they both won travelling scholarships; and in 1938, the last full year of peace, they went off to the continent together. From then on, no matter what, it was a marriage. Like many, perhaps like all, real marriages it had ferocious elements of mutual destruction in it; and, as in other cases, one party was the primary sufferer, but it was utterly indissoluble all the same.

One can just imagine them in Paris before the war. MacBryde, the working-class lad from Maybole wearing the bow-tie that for ever afterwards meant dressing up to him, speaking the French and approving as a revelation the French enjoyment of physical things; Colquhoun dourer and less chameleon-like, more stubborn and perhaps, on the surface at least, more Scots, but enjoying himself all the same. They went to the south, to Aix and Avignon; and they went on into Italy, to Venice and Florence and Rome, sitting in cafés, looking at paintings, liberated. Whatever was between them, the totality cannot help but have been, in some ways anyway, marvellous. And there was one strange circumstance: in those days they did not drink. They were not teetotallers; they took a glass of wine or two; but the serious drinking was to come much later.

They were in Paris when the war broke out and towards the end of the year they returned to Scotland. The idyll was over, but London was to come; and in London, in the forties, they were both successes, Colquhoun driving an ambulance by day and painting by night; MacBryde entertaining on Sunday mornings in the big, bright studio in Notting Hill Gate, to which came Dylan and Sidney Graham and others as well as the painters.

Up to this point success, in decent enough measure, had come their way, as well as friendship and patronage; indeed in the forties the Roberts were, with John Minton, Keith Vaughan, Ayrton and Craxton, among the most praised of that generation of English painters who were known as the English romantics and were the publicised younger names of the day. It was not, of course, to last. They belonged to a generation in which it didn't; and apart from any blockages and the tendency to self-destruction they shared with the other war-babies, there is, in our society at least, perhaps in all, and for all but the most affluent of painters, a dependence on outside factors, on the laws of supply and demand. Colquhoun's last Lefevre show was in 1951, the year before I first met them; and by the time we resumed our acquaintance, in the mid-fifties, it was arguable that nobody much wanted their work anyway. Certainly, whatever its motives, the gallery apparently displayed no enthusiasm about giving him another one. Fashions, by the mid-fifties, had changed; it was the era of 'the kitchen sink' in England, if anybody remembers that, and to occlude matters, it was also the beginnings of abstract expressionism there. 'The English romantics' belonged to the war and immediate post-war. They were old hat.

Every artist who has had an early success, or even some shadow of one, knows the ebb and flow of such things, and the experience of having to soldier on without the sort of attention one got at the beginning, while doing in fact more important and interesting work, is known to many. The Roberts, like others, could have survived the fact that those who are lucky enough to make any sort of news at all—and the luck aspect of it is often debatable—in our Sunday newspaper culture, can only make that sort of news once; indeed such was their resilience that they could have survived a lot more than that. They were called upon, however, to survive pressures, interior and exterior, and indeed, when it was a bit too late—for these things are more easily survived in the earlier years—deprivations and degradations such as fall to the lot of few. In fact when I met them again they had sunk in a few brief years below the point where painting was any longer circumstantially possible. Within that short space of time they had progressed from the lavish bills and late settlements, the rounds of beef and bottles of whiskey at Tilty, not to mention the civilised life of earlier years, to practically complete destitution.

Drink had perhaps something to do with this, for they were both, now, heavy drinkers, and as in many marriages where both parties are so, it had become almost a necessary ingredient in their relationship. But this sort of thing can happen without drink, or without extreme drinking, even if such surprising transitions are rare in the lives of more prudent artists, who have the same desire for security as the bourgeoisie. When their paintings were not wanted any more (and most of Colquhoun's had come back from the last Lefevre show) they had simply used up whatever sources of money were available to them and they had no ability to get any more, even if their paintings had become wanted again, for it can also happen that a painter can find himself suddenly, like any nineteenth-century tradesman, without the minimum requirements in the way of utensils, subsistence money and premises. It must be remembered that most artists in England do, or did still in the fifties, come from the middle- or upper-class strata of society where there is generally private money knocking about, at least in periods of emergency, and that even now those who do not, generally have overtly commercial talents more flexible than the Roberts.

But the fact was that in the circumstances in which they were living now, work would in any case have been impossible, for they now occupied the first of the miserable series of furnished rooms in which the next two or three years were to be dragged out. The lady who owned the house had, a short while before, while the Roberts were safely in the country, been in the habit of declaring herself passionately in love with Colquhoun. Though she seemed less enamoured now, she had rashly offered them accommodation, and then, presumably with some dismay, had discovered that they were quite penniless and unable to pay any rent. There was a large communal kitchen in this house, where those who rented rooms cooked their own meals at whatever time of day it suited them. The food they ate was kept in a big cupboard down there, each person having a named and neatly labelled area of shelf on which stood, in packets and jars, his or her tea, coffee, butter, sugar, bread, carrots, garlic, patna rice, prunes and assorted health foods. The atmosphere was, in general, progressive-bohemian, but it was moneyed progressive-bohemian and very English. Nobody helped themselves to anybody else's health foods, nor did the lady who had once loved Colquhoun provide any. This was not, I believe, because her passion, not having been really reciprocated, had cooled, or because MacBryde was there as well. It was rather a matter of principle. Being English and progressive, she believed that the Roberts should be made to contrive their own arrangements in some way, as a matter both of morality and discipline. Besides, when she found herself, after the first few weeks, unable to recover any rent, she was truly cast down as, being English and progressive, she was usually a stickler for it.

In fact the Roberts had arrived at the point of having absolutely no money whatever, apart from what they might pick up in Soho during the course of the day, and they were therefore reduced to the expedient of taking a pick here and a pick there, two carrots from one place, a scrap of patna rice from another, a small portion of a packet of Muesli from another—not a patch on porridge according to Mac-Bryde—when the kitchen was empty and they judged the coast was clear. Since everybody, including the progressive landlady, went to work, this was not too difficult, though nerve-racking.

On most days, however, they refused to bend themselves to this degrading procedure and would go instead straight to Soho. They would go first to the French pub where they would invest whatever they had in the way of openers. At three o'clock closing they would repair to the old Caves de France, a long dark, rather Spartan bar just up the road which had a club licence and was frequented by a very various lot of people, many of them of distinction. They were not always penniless. MacBryde would make telephone calls to old friends or acquaintances which sometimes bore fruit. For one quite long period there was a number of Colquhoun monotypes down in the cellar of the Caves and there might be the occasional sale of one of these. There were richer denizens of Soho, people who parted regularly on a sort of patronage principle. There were occasional windfalls, as indeed a rather sad one when John Minton died and left them a couple of hundred. But whatever they got, they mostly tended to get in the pubs, when they were already abroad for the day, and it was never enough to change their circumstances, or to change them for long enough for a new beginning that had any chance of bringing with it a possibility of work to be made. They were bound to a diurnally revolving Ixion's wheel which brought them down to the pubs every day, and this, with intervals, was to govern their lives for the next several years.

Not that the Roberts ever could or did descend to certain levels of public-house indignity. MacBryde generally contrived to have something for the mornings; indeed it was often his last care at night, so that they could buy at least their own opening drinks to begin with. After that there were usually enough people about to look after them, and even if the company was not always of the best, it was seldom positively objectionable, nor did they make any more conscious concessions to it than normal affability in a social situation would demand.

And they had a fundamental trait: whenever they had more than the minimal amount of money they were princely with is, particularly to those at that moment poorer than themselves. I have noticed this to be true of all the Scots I have met. However the notion that the Scots are a parsimonious people grew up I do not know: I can only presume it to be another English libel on one of their subject races. In any case when the Roberts became destitute it was too late for them ever to acquire the real ingrowings of the condition. They were used to having money, and when they had it, they spent it.

The trouble with this way of life was not only that it made work impossible, which it did of course, if simply because once launched for the day they were unlikely to return home again, no matter what the circumstances, but it increased their dependence, not only on alcohol, but on the equally insidious and related drug of merely being in company. If they were forced regularly to the pub to begin with, after a while it became an unbreakable habit.

MacBryde had, and retained to the end, a capacity to abandon himself gently and totally to the drink and the moment, so that in the right company he achieved incandescence. He had a beautiful voice and a repertoire of Scots songs and he was seldom reluctant to perform. The voice had originally been a light Scots tenor; now, though the pitch was perfect, it was so gone that the singing had to be a triumph of the dramatic art or nothing: part speech, part mere feeling, backed by an extraordinary sort of mime. Most of the songs were Robert Burns'—also of course an Ayrshire man; much of the wording was inaccurate, but he had filled it out for himself over the years with verses which, though they were often almost meaningless, yet were fitting, even somehow deeply moving. Colquhoun, who was perhaps rendered the unhappier of the two by the inability

138

to work, unfortunately got drunker and got so earlier. As MacBryde said, he 'wooed the drunkenness'; certainly sought a form of oblivion from drink; and got early into that state of wordless inarticulateness which many alcoholics assume but which he liked to assume anyway because he was in fact a very shy and inarticulate man.

In those days the afternoon clubs used to empty out fairly abruptly when the pubs opened at half past five and it was generally MacBryde's custom then to go off on his own, leaving Colquhoun behind. He would go back to the French pub, over to the Swiss or The Duke of Wellington, or even up to the Colony Rooms, which occupied the first floor of a building beside the Caves and was patronised by a somewhat smarter type of customer, film people, queer businessmen, the more commercially successful sort of Soho writer, or the painters who were denizens to some extent of the *haut monde*, Lucien Freud, Francis Bacon or John Minton. By the time they met again both of them were usually fairly drunk, and, for some reason, perhaps because his thoughts had been only of 'ma lover' as he always called him, MacBryde was usually also angry, for it can happen that if we think of somebody intensely enough and with whatever tenderness in their absence, when we meet them again we are likely to pick a quarrel. He would come into the Caves, now filling up with its evening custom, and look about for Colquhoun. After maybe buying himself a drink or accepting one he would stand at the counter muttering. Colquhoun meanwhile might be dancing or flopping about from group to group as he often did, or perched on a stool articulating whichever one of his phrases pleased him best for the time being. MacBryde would then go over and start the attack. The terms of this rarely varied: Presbyterianism, puritanism, the ladies, something which I never understood about east coasters. There might even be violence; MacBryde kicking, Colquhoun making large clumsy gestures to push him away.

Even from the tolerant Caves one or other would some-times have to go, and the separation for the night was often then final. The charge about 'the la-adies' (for the vowel was always prolonged) was a frequent one and made both with a particular viciousness and with some justification, for Colquhoun was susceptible to advances and advances were frequent. I have already referred to the lady who let out rooms and who affected to be deeply smitten by him, but in truth the number of women who were so afflicted was very large. In most cases it appeared to be a genuine emotion, but of course it afflicted particularly the sort of women, and they are numerous, who consciously or otherwise want obstacles and complications set between their passion and its happy fulfilment. There was, first of all, Robert's alleged homosexuality. This was an obstacle that could be, and fairly frequently was, overcome, at least in some circumstances and for an hour or two. There was also his drinking, to which much the same considerations applied, but here a form of kidnapping might be necessary. Once indeed, while the Roberts were still in the country, their subsequent landlady had discovered him drunk and sleeping in the Caves de France. She called a taxi and, under the cloak of a general kindness, had the still half-sleeping Colquhoun conveyed to it by the doorman and other helpers. Having got him home she put him to bed. According to MacBryde at two o'clock in the morning she proceeded to wake the poor man out of his drunken sleep and to offer him, apparently as an aphrodisiac, anchovy sandwiches, when of course all he wanted was drink and company.

These two obstacles aside, there was the fact of MacBryde, his watchfulness and his jealousy. It was sometimes a subject of discussion among some of Colquhoun's acquaintance whether he was 'genuinely' homosexual or not. There were even those who, perhaps liking divisions, said that he was not and never had been, that he had met MacBryde at a formative age, and being shy and awkward with women, had accepted warmth, affection and perhaps sensuality where he found it: though to put it this way is certainly to give it a more plausible psychological gloss than did some who spoke like this. Although as open as the day is long, he was highly reticent. When very drunk he would stagger round the Caves de France saying to whatever girls were present what must have been the sort of things the really shocking lads had said to the girls at Kilmarnock High School so many years before. 'What colour are yer bloomers?' he would enquire, leaning from the perpendicular in what was meant to be an aggressive way; and, 'I want ma hole', he would roar; after which, as often as not, he would double up with amusement at his own effrontery. Other than in the course of these advances he never adverted to the subject of sex. I doubt very much whether in fact he discussed it a great deal with himself. MacBryde may have been right about the puritanism he went on about so often in drink. A gentleman may or may not be a puritan also, and if he is God help him, but he is always a covered well. What is certain is that he needed MacBryde as few people I have known have needed another, and the need was mutual. They may have been instrumental in each other's destruction; MacBryde may have been more instrumental in Colquhoun's than vice versa –the feminine principle usually is–MacBryde's need may have been different, more sexual, in the broadest sense, and perhaps, indeed almost certainly, more sensual, but need it was on both sides, and the sort of need does not really matter, only its degree. 'The one *sine qua non* being mutual need', Auden says, nor if the object of the need is a destroyer does it really matter either, the need must still be fulfilled. The trouble with need marriages is that they are like alcohol–the need creates the need, and where, as often, there is an element of weakness on both sides, or an element of self-destruction, the cycle can be the very devil, for the troubles and terrors mutually created in the first place only lead to greater dependence and so on. In the case of two people as fond of drink as the Roberts, and with as many creative blocks, the cycle was easily attained and, once in motion, its continuance was almost assured. If it happened that the Roberts did get separated in this way and one or other of them wound up at a party and stayed where he was for the night, the telephoning would begin early in the morning and would go on until it was established where the other was and whether he was all right. Marriage is indeed a funny state of being.

Living as they did in fairly dire circumstances, they were not loath to stay elsewhere when the occasion offered, as, frequently when we lived in Camden Town, we would all go down to the old Falcon in the mornings. The mornings were very gentle. It was then that you heard all about the tinker MacBrydes and Aunt Maggie, and something about the early days in the Glasgow School of Art and the studio in Notting Hill Gate. In his book, *On To Timbuctoo*, my friend Anthony Carson described a gathering in Camden Town which included a group of furiously quarrelling Scots painters whom he calls 'the eight McGregors' and he remarks on his astonishment when in the morning 'the eight McGregors turned out to be as peaceful as purling mountain brooks.'

Fairly shortly after I met them again I got a job as literary editor of a famous old weekly called *Time and Tide*, then the lagging third of the trio once composed of the *New Statesman*, *The Spectator* and itself. In the twenties and thirties, *Time and Tide* had been a liberal and progressive enough journal. It was also strongly feminist, indeed it was known irreverently as 'Sapphic's Graphic'. Although it was still edited by its founder Lady Rhondda, only the feminism remained. It was now the favourite journal of the fevered swamps of imperial reaction round Cheltenham and Bath, and the organ of those Tory journalists and politicians who had philosophies of Conservatism. There was no Enoch Powell in those days: Lord Salisbury was the beau ideal.

I was unfortunate in that my term of office, if that is what it should be called, coincided with the controversy over the ending of capital punishment, the Suez crisis and other matters on which the paper took a strongly reactionary stand. This did not matter ethically, for the book pages were the book pages, and, after all, if a Tory like John Raymond could work for the *New Statesman* I should have been able to for *Time and Tide*. But the unfortunate thing is that I am a reactionary too; the atmosphere of the office, which was staffed mostly by débutantes or girls who wished they had been, was either febrile with Tory enthusiasm or resonant with Tory despair; and in this ambience and these circumstances my left-wing hackles, rendered rather dormant by working on *The Bell* under Peadar, began to rise. I reacted.

And then there was the editor. Lady Rhondda was a woman of considerable personality and, indeed, considerable achievement. Further she gave one, in certain respects, a moderately free hand. But she was old, so old that the paper was almost edited by a system of wheels and pulleys, and though this meant frequent absences on her part, her flexibility was gone. A painting of her in earlier years wearing a velvet jacket and floppy tie hung on the wall in the room next door to mine. When Colquhoun saw it he said: 'Ah. R-rupert Br-rooke!' It was not an inapt association. There was a particular class of contributor known as 'an old friend of the paper' and these had to be given certain books, while their own books must be reviewed and could not be attacked. There had also grown up, under the junta of debs who had managed the book pages in the interval between the editorships of John Betjeman and myself, a system of advice and control. Political books must be referred to so and so, biographies to a peer of the realm who was also a director of the paper. These gentlemen were in the habit of dropping in and it proved hard to circumvent them. There were also the regular reviewers who could not be displaced, and, though some of these were eminent and learned enough, they were certainly not notorious for irreverence or attack; in contemporary parlance they were neither with-it, nor trendy: they were not members of the *avant-garde*: and though disapproving of much that was regarded as with-it and trendy in those far off days when the words were unheard of, I would have liked more irreverence, more attack and more wit. After all I had been weaned on the school of *Horizon* and the *New Statesman*.

For all these reasons my heart was only fitfully in the job. But enough. This is not an autobiography, either personal or professional, and I say all this simply to explain why, apart from basic temperamental reasons, I tended to spend more time with the ruined men of Soho, in Soho, rather than in Bloomsbury or literary London in general, if such a thing exists. Certainly I only fitfully responded to such invitations to the other clubland as came my way, nor apart from my own importations, who were people I was acquainted with already, and in fact belonged mostly to the *milieu* I have described, were the staff or the contributors to *Time and Tide* such as one would normally see much of outside the office.

And whatever mode of success I desired, it was closer to the sort that the ruined men aspired to than to that which apparently filled the dreams of most of my English poetic contemporaries. In Soho the standards which had made the true *avant-garde* art of the century were represented, even if only by casualties of the assault.

I suppose what I am trying to say really is that whatever possibilities of success as literary editor, man of letters, reviewer, critic, or whatnot were open to me did not fit the archetypal patterns created by the lonely and suffering geniuses who had made the great art of our time. The ruined men of Soho did that.

8

ONE AFTERNOON as I sat in my room, known as the bookroom in *Time and Tide,* weighed down or otherwise by the cares of office, a friend of mine rang up to say that he was round the corner in The Horseshoe with Julian Maclaren-Ross, who would like to meet me. Had I ever heard of Julian Maclaren-Ross? Had I indeed! In the days when the world of contemporary letters was represented almost entirely by *Penguin New Writing* and an odd copy of *Horizon* I had read the acerbic, brittle, funny stories, sometimes with tiny shrugged-off undertones of loneliness and pain, which had appeared in those journals under that name. The war was on but even in far-off Ireland I could sense their truth, for the kingdom of misrule has no boundaries and was as real to me in boarding school as it appeared to be to the author in the British Army. Besides, the technique of the stories was so spare and unerring as to constitute, in however small a way, almost a new kind of writing. They were also very funny and had, to my schoolboy eyes at least, the unmistakable shine of the *avant-garde*. They contributed to establishing, indeed they almost created, for me at least, the mode of the day.

The figure that confronted me in The Horseshoe, however, seemed to personify several different modes and eras at once. He wore a belted, fawn overcoat that suggested the fast thirties and a polo-necked sweater which hinted at a different *persona* of the same decade, but he carried a gold-topped cane which was definitely Edwardian, as was the manner, consisting of 'dear boys' and 'you young men' and 'people of my age'. The accent was grating, with r's that never quite rolled and s's that did not quite constitute a lisp. I surmised

145

that it belonged rather to the twenties, but whatever it was, it was not quite pukka, rather something that might once have been imagined, by Michael Arlen or some other star-struck outsider, to be so.

As with eras, so with professions and modes of being. There were strange little *revenants,* some of them only to become apparent as our acquaintance developed, of the Edwardian masher, the public school man turned door-to-door carpet seller, the Riviera playboy, the sex maniac on Brighton pier, the genius spurned by Wardour Street, even the disdainful literary man, keeping editors at bay. And somewhere behind them all there was perhaps the penniless highland gentleman, blood soured and impulses twisted by the unfortunate experiences of several generations at inferior English schools, but ready in the final reckoning to settle matters with the rapier. As I got to know Julian better I discovered that he was in fact an actor first and foremost, an actor of the old school who had imagined himself perman-ently into certain roles, which he relished with a somewhat seedy zest.

That afternoon I had brought along a book to offer him for review: I was, after all, trying to introduce more sophis-tication into the book pages. He accepted it somewhat disdainfully, seeming to think that I should have written to him or something first, but he was otherwise very cordial, praising two pieces I had written, both, as it happened, attacks on then fashionable authors, and asking me, for some reason, if I had thought of writing an attack on a dead writer who was having a strong posthumous run. Since in fact I thought the reputation in question was an inflated one, this did not seem like a bad idea, but I was a bit mystified when he began in his rasping voice with the swallowed 'r's to sketch out my plan of campaign for me. There was, it seemed, a book about the writer in question coming out. I should ask Pryce-Jones if I might do a middle for the T.L.S. and 'finish him off'. Of course it would not be signed, so I would get no public recognition for it, 'but everybody in the trade will know who wrote it' and there were 'a lot of people waiting to see the end of him'. This was not my impression; and besides, I had no intention of being anybody else's junior hatchetman. What was his animus? I tried to find out, but I had to be content with the statement that there were a great many things I would learn as I went along.

Whatever his reservations about accepting a book in a pub, two days later the review arrived in the post, accompanied by a request for cash in his extraordinarily neat calligraphy. Later the same day the rasping voice came on the telephone. He was quite broke, and he would like, if possible, to have the fee, or an advance on it, immediately. I understood the urgency of course, and I tried to explain as best I could from my office chair that *Time and Tide* was a stodgy journal, most of whose contributors were as a class rather stodgy people, not indigent literary men like ourselves; that there was no procedure for getting money in advance of publication nor indeed for a week after that, and that there was nothing I could do. He became quite high and mighty immediately and told me that Pryce-Jones, Le-eh-hmann, Spender and Anthony Powell were all accustomed to pay him immediately on delivery of his copy. If these men would do it, why not I? I explained again. He insisted that I must at least try and that I should meet him in The Golden Lion in Dean Street at half past five. I didn't try. I had tried before, and knew it was no use. The ways of accountants are more wonderful than the things that man may know. But I went along to The Golden Lion.

He was coatless and stickless. The stick was in pawn. So was his gold fountain-pen, like the stick an heirloom from his father. He could not write without the pen so that 'even if a commission turned up I would now be unable to fulfil it'. He appeared to be quite cheerful, however, and was drinking 'bhra-a-ndy'. I had expected reproaches but he brushed my apologies about the money aside quite amicably and discoursed about his past and his plans. I began to learn another thing about Julian, of whom I was by now quite fond: like most professional story-tellers, he was a great bore. The boredom was, however, embellished by rococo flourishes which, if they did not enliven the proceedings, raised the tone of it. As a bore, he had style, and there was the interest of the gallery of characters which he played: indeed, as in the case of the sort of old-fashioned actor I have compared him to, there was the interest of the non-conceal-ment of his own flamboyance within each role. The roles might change rapidly: the voice and gestures were the same. The sex maniac and the great film director both gestured and declaimed in the same way.

He explained that even if I had had the money he could on no account have come to the office to collect it. I would have had to bring it to the pub. When he came to London first he had made it a rule never to meet publishers, agents, editors or such people in their offices, their clubs or wherever, but always in the pub. 'Of course in those days I had the whip hand. Sansom and I were quite as famous as all these Wains and Amises and people are now. Mind you there wasn't as much paper about in those days, so we didn't get as much publicity and we didn't do as well financially. But then I was writing films.' I had heard a lot about 'those days' from various friends. How Julian had stood nightly in The Fitzroy or The Wheatsheaf with his stick on the counter, the centre of an admiring circle over which he presided with great haughtiness, and I was curious. What in fact had happened to him since?

I remembered that shortly after the war he had published the first two volumes of a projected trilogy: *The Weeping and the Laughter* and *Bitten by the Tarantula*. My horizons were then broadening somewhat, but I remembered also being surprised that one of the central figures in the world of the *avant-garde* magazines should get such rather off-hand treatment from the reviewers.

I couldn't of course ask directly what had happened in the intervening years for that would be to suggest that he had been entirely inactive, while in fact at that very moment he was full of his present plans and future schemes. But in the course of conversation I discovered something else about him: he liked the myth of apparent failure; forms of revenge intrigued him and forms of mysterious return; the ruined gambler with one last throw, the heir who would reappear one stormy night, the Jacobite exile who would live to see the usurpers humbled. This was something in his own character, but it had another dimension. He belonged, like so many of the friends and acquaintances I had made in Soho, to the ruined generation, that which had arrived during the war. Like the Roberts, like Paul Potts, like even, in his famous way, Dylan Thomas, he was a ruined man to begin with, someone for whom the conditions, the very nature of success and non-success had been altered by public calamity. He was a north Soho, nineteen-forties baby.

In the course of the drinking it transpired in a sort of high-handed way that he had been staying in a cheap hotel in Bloomsbury, but that he had been put out of it that morning and had now no place to go. It seemed to happen often and he didn't make a fuss about it. It was a fact of circumstance, interesting more because of the iniquity and treachery of the hotel management than anything else; and he did not ask me if I could put him up, but all the same I offered to.

At this time I lived with my wife and small baby in a lower middle-class suburb in Wembley. Evidently built some time in the nineteen-thirties, it was a wasteland of identical roads and grey houses, Tudor by virtue of boards stuck in the concrete. It stretched for miles in every direction. We were there by an accident of fortune, but that is another story; suffice it to say that we occupied the ground floor of one of these innumerable 'villas', the rest being occupied by a spinster lady who read books for Boots's library and her mother, a deaf and house-bound old lady who was over ninety. The ground floor where we were had been occupied until her recent death by another old lady, cousin or something of the one upstairs, and of the things that remained as a sign of her occupation one was a large, gloomy and forbidding family Bible.

I put Julian to bed on a couch in the little, over-furnished, mortuary-like front sitting-room that we never used, and some time during the night he found the Bible. He apparently stayed up reading it, and in the morning, when he heard me moving about, he came out in a high state of excitement with the Bible in his hand. He had, it appeared, made several discoveries. These were not, it seemed, orthodox theological revelations; they were illuminations of the psychology of someone called Selena (pronounced by Julian Sel-eh-nya). You only had to cut the Bible and you found

149

out what Sel-eh-nya was thinking of you. There followed some demonstrations, not unconvincing if you put the lady mentioned in the position of the Lord, stand-offish, but jealous and vengeful all the same, and therefore of course secretly interested.

But who was Sel-eh-nya? She was the girl he loved. She occupied his every waking thought. One enquired about the circumstances and gathered that the girl in question had been married to the fellow-writer Julian had wanted me to attack and that she had been secretary to a literary magazine, the sort of charmingly competent girl who in those circum-stances often does much of the editing; indeed her glamour for Julian, I began to suspect, perhaps unworthily, had something to do with these facts, but I never got beyond them into the realm of actual meetings, assignations, even reciprocated signals. Was this passion returned? In the discourse that followed it was difficult to make out. One got as far as 'You see Sel-eh-nya thinks I'm one of those bohemians', or 'Sel-eh-nya thinks I'm finished' or 'A lot of people have told her a lot of things about me', and there would follow intimations of obscure vengeances, sudden appearances, daring coups, turnings of tables, even hints of abduction or worse. It would seem that through the agency of others, not quite identifiable, the general opinion that Sel-eh-nya held of him was something like the one Caroline Lamb had of Byron. She was of course fascinated, but afraid.

At this very moment he was writing a film scenario to be called 'Until the Day She Dies' about a girl (Selena) who was secretly aware of the interest taken in her by a sinister stranger on a motor-cycle (himself). The sinister stranger was obsessed by the girl and would eventually murder her, in fact the remaining days of her life were numbered on a calendar which would punctuate the film. She seemed somehow to be aware of this and to find the prospect exciting.

When I went off to *Time and Tide* he was sitting at the kitchen table, elaborating on the incidents of the story to my wife. When I returned in the evening he was still at it. Thérèse was listening in a sort of stunned silence and the kitchen table was now covered with sheets of paper representing the posters for the movie, the titles and the credits, all scrupulously designed down to the last detail. It was also fully cast and a director had been appointed. Julian himself of course filled the leading role and it seemed that he went around in leather togs, helmet, gauntlets and goggles most of the time. When not wearing these, he was wearing dark glasses; he had a limp and he carried a stick. Selena herself of course was not competent to play the female lead: that part, I remember, was awarded to Glynis Johns.

He had discarded the shirt in which he had arrived and was now wearing a Cornish fisherman's jersey which had been given to me by a lady I knew. Too small for me, it was several sizes too small for him, but my picture of him during the next week or so is of a tall, angular figure, usually standing at the telephone in the hall, with neck and arms sticking out of the jersey, tirelessly haranguing somebody at the end of the line. The telephone calls began early and continued during that part of the day not occupied by recapitulations and further inventions to do with 'Until The Day She Dies'. They were mostly to agents, film producers, publishers and their offices. His manner with the girls through whom calls were channelled was haughty, not to say aggressive, or even insulting, so that he did not really get very far towards the ostensible purpose of any call, and frequently the object of the exercise seemed to be to have a good run in with subordinates. It was on foot of the telephone calls that he had had the first of several clashes with the lady upstairs who read for Boots's library. The telephone was shared in an uneasy sort of way, as was the hall; and Julian, like too many of us, had no respect for his host's difficulties of circumstance. There was no use asking him to be nice to her. His own preoccupations came first and to her this tall, genuinely sinister figure, clad in an ill-fitting fisherman's jersey, rasping away loudly and endlessly at obscure enemies, discovering everywhere plots against his interests and denials of his rights, delivering himself of ferocious if some- what indefinite threats often in the name of a certain 'Mr. Hyde', must have seemed a strange visitation, perhaps even, to her life and her mother's, a danger. During the week, however, a minor miracle occurred, one of the few I have ever known of this particular variety. As a bonus for her services she was accustomed to receive bundles of throwouts from Boots. One arrived; it contained *The Weeping and The Laughter*. She began to read it. She was charmed; and from there on nothing could be too good for Mr. Maclaren-Ross, who, be it said to his credit, responded with mirthless, seigniorial smiles and bows which she seemed to find perfectly acceptable, though I must confess that if I had been her they would have chilled me to the marrow.

Meanwhile the saga of Selena continued; and never, it is safe to say, was a grand passion unfolded for the listener with such a strange lack of circumstance included in the unfolding. When you could shift Julian on to such cheerful subjects as an Edgar Wallace play he had seen in the twenties in which there was a representation of an actual hanging on the stage, or the sense of evil conveyed by Sidney Greenstreet in *The Maltese Falcon*, he could be quite good company, but because of the lack of facts, the grand passion was not the most entertaining of topics.

Meanwhile, he stayed, and stayed in the house too, for beyond its confines he would not budge. Once, on a beautiful sunny, early spring day, Thérèse lured him out into the little, bare front garden to see a solitary crocus that was struggling up, but he fled back indoors immediately, declaring that for a lover like himself the sight was too sad. On another occasion we left him to baby-sit while we went out. When we came back about midnight he was standing in the doorway with the baby in his arms, both of them in a state of panic. 'She's wet. She's wet, I tell you. There's something wrong,' he kept saying. It appeared that the baby had woken up howling. In attempting to find out what was the matter Julian had discovered that her nappy was wet and this had seemed to him evidence that there was something gravely wrong. He had been standing at the door for half-an-hour, with the baby in his arms, hoping to get aid or advice from a passerby.

He had of course no money and therefore he could not leave. In spite of my style and titles I was really paid very little, and though I supplemented that little by the judicious flogging of unreviewed books, I had to be careful about this as the principle of the thing had never been established by my predecessors: indeed apart from John Betjeman I had no real predecessors, the literary editing having been mostly done by the débutantes with which *Time and Tide* abounded, charming girls who flogged only the occasional gardening book of which they had scrupulously written a 'shorter notice'—in theory the proceeds of the surplus books were supposed to go to some feminist trust or other. I therefore could not float Julian off into the world again with a grant-in-aid—nor indeed would I have asked him to leave even if I could have given him money.

A long week-end—I think the Whit—supervened during which we all sat around. There was even less money than usual in the house. Julian would drink neither tea, coffee nor beer, contenting himself with plain water. It was a trying time for us all, and this though he attempted to keep our spirits up by leading us in prayers to Selena—'She is kind at heart. She will send money.'

Then on the Tuesday the man of action took over and one of the telephone calls bore fruit. It was to Anthony Powell in *Punch* and it was arranged that there should be a book for collection and review, with immediate payment for the result. The trouble was of course that he could not write without his gold fountain-pen, which was in a pawnshop off Gray's Inn Road. However, I flogged some books and that evening I brought home the money for the pen. Next day, while I was at work, Thérèse travelled into town, collected the pen and the book and brought them both back. Julian reviewed the book there and then at the kitchen table —it was *The Man In The Grey Flannel Suit,* a well-publicised masterpiece of the era—and Thérèse took off for town again, this time to Fleet Street to deliver the review and collect the cheque. Arrangements had been made for this to be cashable in the office, so she was able to return with actual money. When I came home Julian repaid me the money for the pen and I accompanied him to the station. I remember being impressed by the amount of money *Punch* was apparently willing and able to pay for a couple of hundred words.

At the pub near the station the affluent senior man of letters took over. He insisted on br-ahndies and then declared that under no circumstances would he go on the tube. 'That kind of thing is all very well for you young men starting out, but it won't do for chaps like me. I've been in the game a long time and I'm too old for that sort of thing.' So, in spite of the appalling distance to London, a taxi had to be fetched, and in it he at length departed.

The following night, very late, the telephone rang. I had a terrible premonition, so I lifted the receiver off the hook and pressed it to my ear, saying nothing. 'Hello, Cronin? This is Maclaren-Ross here,' said the well-known voice. I hate to confess this, but at that stage I placed the receiver gently on the table and covered it with a rug.

About a week later I met Julian in the Caves de France. He was standing by the bar sipping a glass of wine, and he had his gold-topped stick and his musical comedy star overcoat on, so I knew he was relatively prosperous. He was also wearing a pair of dark glasses in which, because of some mirror property of the lens, the other person could see only himself.

'I am Mr. Hyde today. You must call me Mr. Hyde,' he said. Then he turned to the barman, Secundo Carnera, and called out haughtily, 'Have there been any messages for Mr. Hyde?'

'No, Joolian, no. No messages for Meester Hyde so far,' replied Carnera, that most accommodating of men.

It appeared that he became Mr. Hyde when he was feeling particularly vengeful or sinister.

He told me that he had rung up a few nights before, but that he had been cut off for some reason and couldn't get through again. I made clicking noises with my tongue and asked him what he had done. 'Oh I slept on a bench in Wembley Park', he replied.

Naturally I was shocked and repentant, though I did not tell him so. I had had no idea he was in Wembley when he rang, having travelled all the way out: in fact I had thought he was still in town; and though I knew he was going to ask to be put up, we were all at the end of our tether. He treated the matter very matter of factly, however, as I would have done myself. Literary men who have led more sheltered lives might reflect that he was at this time in his middle or late forties; that, whatever the merits of his work, he had been, after a fashion, a success; and that, whatever its merits, his work was still remembered and respected. This life pattern, I thought, was more suited to a poet than a mere prose writer; for a mere prose writer it was almost magnificent. But of course he belonged to the doomed generation.

Some time later, by a happy chance, I met the woman of his dreams. Finding that she had a sense of humour I approached the subject of Julian, but cautiously. She said she did not know him very well and she appeared not to realise the extent of his obsession. Remembering the mad motor-cyclist and the calendar on which the days of her life were numbered, I even wondered whether I ought not to warn her. I made some little joke about how important she was to him. She said, yes, she had heard from other people he had a crush on her, but she had only really met him once, very briefly, when she had shared a taxi with him to or from a dinner someone gave in a restaurant. He had asked her to dinner himself on that occasion, but she didn't turn up or he didn't turn up, she couldn't remember. Of course she had met him once or twice when she had been secretary of the magazine, but that was ages ago and he had given no indication of nourishing a grand passion then. All in all, I decided there was no need to mention the mad motor-cyclist.

Often when one met him in Soho and elsewhere he was being Mr. Hyde, with the stick and the dark glasses, and one was forbidden, on pain of displeasure, to call him anything else. The sex maniac was well to the fore in this role, but the previous obsession was less and less mentioned. He was, it seemed, 'in the hands of a tall girl'. Sometimes she was trying to kill him. 'But she won't succeed. I'm stronger than she is, you see. I'm taller too, though she is tall, very tall. But that's why I'm being Mr. Hyde today, you see. Because she's trying to kill me.'

Eventually, to everybody's surprise, he got married and he had a new lease of life of a sort after that, as a radio script writer. *Until The Day She Dies* had been metamorphosed into an apparently endless afternoon Light Programme serial. I even heard a bit of it in a café in Fleet Street one day while the pubs were shut. Julian was playing in it himself and the rasping voice gave me quite a turn. He did not seem to be the murderer, however, but an almost equally mysterious blind pianist. My own occasions sometimes took me about this time to the B.B.C. pubs, The George and The Stag's Head, and I used to see him there, looking somewhat out of place among the Corporation's employees, rather like a scarecrow among seagulls, and acting away in any one of his many, now familiar, roles. He was kept in employment by some old hands who knew who he was, and such was their authority that one writer of poetic Irish features pointed him out to me, saying, 'He's an old has-been, of course, but if the rest of us could write like him we could be very proud of ourselves. He's a very pure writer, very, very pure.'

Meanwhile he led a highly nomadic existence with his wife, and, eventually, a son, who bore the fine Highland name of Alexander. They lived it appeared mostly in hotels and there were often difficulties about the bills. Julian seemed a fond father. I met him one day pushing the pram through Soho and he was in high spirits. He had been reading a novel of Iris Murdoch's and he claimed that the hero-villain was a portrait of himself. 'All these young women put me in their books. They think I'm wicked you see. Of course they put me in disguise, but that doesn't fool me. As you know, Cronin, I'm a master of disguise.'

We had a slight falling-out because he refused to witness for me in a motoring case which had arisen out of driving him home one night, and because of something I said to the prosecuting counsel who had tried to set a trap for me, ponderously working round to the suggestion that there must have been at least six drinks if each of the three men in the company had bought two. 'Oh but you don't realise', I had said, 'Maclaren-Ross never buys his round'. He was mollified though when I told him that the same individual had said to me, 'Let's just call him Ross, shall we, it saves time', and that I had replied, 'I'd rather call him Maclaren-Ross, if you don't mind. You see he's the chief of his clan.' As far as I knew he had never pretended to be that, but I knew he would be pleased to be provided with a new role.

Eventually he and his wife parted. Mr. Hyde seemed more in evidence than ever. He refused one evening we met to come to the Caves De France with me, on the grounds that 'all those noisy Colquhouns and MacBrydes and people' would be in there, and he took me instead to a new club upstairs in Old Compton Street, where customers and staff actually knew him as Mr. Hyde and nothing else. He was very proud of this, laughing his peculiar 'ha-ha-ha' laugh and indulging himself in condescending jokes and conversation with the barmaid, though of course he had no small talk whatever.

The last time I saw him was in The Mandrake late at night. He was with a young woman who was apparently an actress in the B.B.C repertory company. She complained bitterly that she had been asked out to dinner and had now spent four dinnerless hours in the pubs. 'There,' said Julian with immense dignity and supreme seriousness, pointing at the uncatable sandwich which The Mandrake was forced by law to serve with all drinks, 'There is your dinner'.

It was to the wasteland of Wembley that the Roberts came one night after The Mandrake had shut. They were, as often, desperate for a place to prolong the night in and company to forget with. Somehow they got a bottle of whiskey and asked if they could come to Wembley to drink it. It did not seem to me to be much of a prospect for them. Wembley was a long way off. There would be only ourselves, and MacBryde could not do much singing there. But it was a dead night with very few people around; they had nowhere else to go; and I had had a few drinks and was in the mood for more. Unfortunately, until we finally, if ever, gain sense, that's the way of it.

Thérèse was with us and it was agreed that they could stay. They would in any case have no means of getting back. So we got on the tube, Colquhoun carrying the precious bottle, wrapped in brown paper. During the journey he swayed around the swaying carriage, making incomprehensible but evidently humorous advances to various girls. They and their escorts tolerated this because he looked like a big, good-humoured, drunken Scots lad, perhaps a sailor, who was far from home, meant no harm and was not likely to say anything that common morality

157

would deem really offensive. But MacBryde was getting angrier and, apart from anything else, the bottle, in its brown paper covering, was patently in danger.

On the platform at Wembley MacBryde demanded it and after some argument he got it. He went into the jakes, and, suspecting that he might be helping himself to a swig or two, Colquhoun and I followed. Just as we went through the door we heard the unmistakable sound. The bottle was in fragments on the wet floor and the whiskey was running away into the urinal. A moment before we had been in possession of a quantity of amber liquid that automatically meant fellowship, forgetfulness and joy, however foolish. Now we were in Wembley, at one o'clock in the morning with nothing to look forward to but cups of tea. Such is the nature of the irretrievable accident. There was nothing for it now but to face the walk across the common, the ugly drinkless house, and the night before all of us.

I knew there was going to be trouble even before we set off. The recriminations had started. Colquhoun was philosophical enough to begin with, but MacBryde characteristically had moved from defence to attack. It had nothing to do with who was to blame. What bothered him was of course the loss of the whiskey. It had begun to rain heavily and that dampened emotions down a bit, but even in the downpour and the darkness there was talk of 'the la-dies', 'presbyter-erianism', 'east coasters' and 'puritanism'. Colquhoun so far was contenting himself with an odd roar of 'you broke it—you broke the fucking thing' and when we actually got into the suburban road where I lived I was able to prevail on them, briefly, to keep quiet. I was thinking of the lady upstairs who read for Boots's library, and of her mother, however deaf.

In the house we all sat around for a while. Thérèse made tea but nobody drank it. The mutterings continued and once MacBryde made a run at Colquhoun and kicked him. I suggested that we should all go to bed and I did the best I could with a mattress and blankets on the floor of the funereal front room where Julian had slept on the couch. But sleep for any of us was not to be.

After a while MacBryde's voice could be heard in the

familiar pattern of abuse, while Colquhoun let out an odd roar of 'You let the whiskey fall. You broke the fucking thing.' I was certain that the lady upstairs must be able to hear most of this, whatever about her deaf mother. However, the rain and Colquhoun's roarings were now accompanied by loud outbreaks of thunder; giant bangs directly overhead being succeeded by distant mutterings, the whole pattern providing an accompaniment to and indeed somewhat resembling what went on next door.

During one particularly loud interchange I could hear furniture being turned over and I got up to plead and if possible to pacify. They were both standing naked in the middle of the floor, lit by occasional flashes of lightning. Colquhoun had a chair raised over his head and MacBryde was standing in an accusatory attitude in front of him, orating about 'a certain occasion when you went off to pleasure the la-ady'. I knew Colquhoun was not going to use the chair, but I understood the frustration he was suffering and was not surprised when he hurled it down on the floor with a great cry of 'for God's sake, shut up.'

I got them back under the blankets by threats, cajolery and reproach, but I realised it was not going to stop, and as I lay in the next room I could hear between the thunder MacBryde's voice going on and on, until at last Colquhoun began to roar again, sometimes in his agony just letting out great shouts of 'Stop' and 'Shut up.' Finally came one enormous cry and the sounds of a scuffle. As I got up again, in sufficient agony of spirit to do murder myself, I heard them clattering about in the hall and in the kitchen. As I opened the hall door the two bodies went past me. MacBryde was first and he was making for the hall-door. He got it open and vanished out into the rain. Then Colquhoun came after him and he had a carving-knife in his hand.

The houses in this part of Wembley have front gardens typical of their kind: a bit of grass representing a lawn, a rose-bush or two and a few flowers to border the grass and the concrete path. Round and round this tiny enclosure in this lower middle-class suburb in the pouring rain went the two white figures, stark naked, one of them emitting roars to match the thunder's volume and with a carving knife in his hand. Intermittent flashes of lightning lit up the long streamers of rain, the two glistening bodies, the trampled rose-bushes and the faces of terrified neighbours at upstairs windows. They were not to know that it was only a specially dramatic lovers' quarrel and that Colquhoun was the most peaceable of men. All they saw was one naked man being pursued by another who was shouting bloody murder and had a knife raised over his head as if in act to strike. It was therefore no wonder that someone rang for the police.

I was wearing slippers and in desperation I took one off and struck Colquhoun with it. This stopped him and then, as we stood there in the garden, the Roberts with the rain pouring down their bodies, and I in my sopping wet pyjamas, MacBryde changed his tune. 'My lover. Oh my lover', he cried, weeping. 'You attacked him. You attacked him with a slipper. You beat him over the head with a slipper. My lover. My poor lover.' This was grotesquely unjust, but at least it changed the nature of the proceedings and gave some hope of peace.

The door was still open to the rain and wind. I began to urge them through it and into the hall, where so often Julian had stood at the telephone haranguing underlings. A stairs led from this to the upstairs quarters and the moment we got through the door, I knew the worst. There were two figures at the top, clad in nightgowns and swathed in shawls and other garments. It was the lady who read for Boots's library and her mother who was over ninety and had not heard a sound for years. She had heard something tonight, however, whether Colquhoun or the thunder, and now she saw things too. 'Oh my Gawd. Niked. Niked as the day of judgment. And 'e's got a knoife', she cried in the cracked tones of the old, and began to make curious hooting noise over and over again. Fortunately for me, her distress was so great that her daughter hustled her away and explanations were postponed for the time being.

I gave the Roberts towels and got them back to bed before the police arrived, a sergeant and two men with dripping capes and bull's-eye lanterns. I interviewed them in the hall and admitted that two friends of mine, Scots lads on holidays, had been having a bit of frolic. 'They were a bit ebullient,' I said. It is essential, when dealing with the police, to make it either simple or highly sophisticated. But there had been a complaint about a knife, the sergeant said, and it was alleged that there had been a certain amount of indecent exposure. I hotly denied the knife, claiming it was a figment of somebody's imagination. They had been having a wash, I said, and there had been a bit of frolicking. He chewed on this for a moment. 'Where are they now, sir'? he asked. 'Asleep, I hope,' I answered, nodding towards the door of the front room. 'I must see them, sir', he said. I took a chance, in more respects than one, and opened the door for him, MacBryde was sitting up on the mattress, faintly illuminated by a street lamp. He had a shirt on. Colquhoun was lying beside him, peaceful as a lamb. 'Is there ainy sorrt of tr-rooble?' asked MacBryde innocently. 'There has been a complaint,' answered the sergeant, 'and I think for everybody's sake there had better not be any more . . . frolicking tonight.'

Nor was there. In the morning of course there was the usual transformation. The Roberts were 'as peaceful as purling Highland brooks'. I had the lady upstairs to placate but so extraordinary had been the scene and so theatrical the background of the thunder and lightning that I think she was a little uncertain as to whether she and her mother had not somehow dreamt it all. Finding the going easier than I had expected I allowed myself the luxury of satisfying a normal curiosity. Had it been, I delicately enquired, the thunderstorm or my friends that her mother had heard, she who had not heard anything at all for years? It had been, it seemed, my friends.

I was sitting in *Time and Tide* one morning, with, as luck would have it, a hangover ebbing and flowing inside my head, when I had an unexpected telephone call. In order to cool the ardour of certain would-be reviewers of the sort who want to come round every day and eventually to come and live with you, I had asked the girl on the switchboard to enquire for the time being who was calling, a thing I had never done before. In this case she told me that the caller would say only, 'Tell him it's Brendan'. Because the tides of hangover were at that moment beating against the walls of the skull, I did not immediately realise who it was. So I told her to ask again. And, unfortunately, after she had done so, and the same answer had been given, I was still unyielding. Then I got it. My heart sank. I had, if you can have such a thing, visions of diatribes, justified ones too, because if this was an overture and I knew who it was, not taking the call must have seemed what Brendan would describe as 'the act of a bollocks'.

To begin with I was right. When he was put through he said among other things that he was 'a real writer, not like some other people that were supposed to be writers and sat in offices all day'. He did his writing 'with ink and paper, not with telephones and dictaphones'.

There were no dictaphones in *Time and Tide*, but I bore with this, for old times' sake. Then he asked me to meet him for a drink. He was in Ward's Irish House in Piccadilly.

Ward's Irish House is an underground bar, suited to a race of tunnel diggers. Brendan was with his wife and a friend and an illicit bottle of Irish whiskey. This was parked under the table in the alcove where he sat, and poured from every now and then, into the glasses provided by the house for the first drink. The procedure unnerved me. The barmen in Ward's may have been Irish, but I was used to limey legality.

I remember little of the conversation, if there was any conversation. The tides of hangover raged and frothed and I think I may have said a few stupid things. I remember saying something about his having a chip on his shoulder.

Then calamity struck, obliquely, as calamity usually will; and as is usually the case, the extent of the damage was not revealed till later.

Brendan told me he had a play coming on. This was *The Quare Fellow*, though I knew nothing about that. He asked me would I like to go to it.

I asked him when and where it was being produced.

He said, at Stratford.

I said, 'Oh, that's too far away, Brendan. I'd have to take a couple of days off from the paper to go down there.'

Strange though it may seem for a London literary man, which, after my fashion, I was in those days, I had never heard of Miss Joan Littlewood's theatre at Stratford East in the East End of London, and for some reason I thought that a production of some sort was in the offing at Stratford-on-Avon. Stratford East is of course a good way from the normal haunts of West End man, but it is not a day's journey.

Anyway, soon after, the pub closed. There had been no open breach, but there had hardly been anything else either. Still, in spite of my response to the invitation, which must by now have been rankling, when we got outside, Brendan asked me if I would come down to Fleet Street to the Press Club where apparently he had the entrée. I had a perfectly good Club of my own up the road, the Caves de France, and it crossed my mind to suggest it, but I didn't, and so we parted.

A couple of forenoons later I was sitting in the York Minster with two friends when Brendan came in. He had one or two people with him and a bundle of newspapers under his arm. *The Quare Fellow* had been produced at Stratford East the night before and apparently it had been an uproarious success, but not having seen a newspaper I didn't know that either.

I half-waved. Perhaps he expected me to get up and congratulate him—I don't know. If I had read about the play's production and success I would, and indeed, should, have done.

He walked over to the table, apparently selecting with some care one of the papers from under his arm. Reaching us, he flung it down in front of me, knocking over my glass. It was the *Daily Express* and it carried quite a spread about him. He had evidently taken some care that this should be right side up, legible and visible to me. There followed a diatribe, long and detailed, about some University contemporaries I had published in *The Bell*; about my bogman and bourgeois origins; and, for some reason, about my relationship with Kavanagh. Then he picked up his paper, collected his companions and, surprisingly, walked out of the pub.

My friends, to whom the diatribe had been wonderful but incomprehensible, asked me who that was.

'His name is Brendan Behan,' I said.
'Ah,' they said, 'the famous Brendan Behan'.
For unbeknownst to me, the years of fame had begun.

Later that week he was drunk on the television with Malcolm Muggeridge and, in a sense beyond jest, his doom was accomplished. Wherever one went from now on, every other newspaper would contain photographs of an ever more bloated Brendan, apparently endlessly performing a clumsy *danse macabre* for an avid audience. The nadir, I thought, was a *Picture Post* interview in which he compared himself with Dylan Thomas; prophesied for himself an early death and suggested that this was somehow the fate of an artist of his ilk. He was evidently living through a newspaper nightmare.

There may, indeed there must have been more to it than that, but from the outside it certainly seemed that the society he affected to despise had him by the short hairs and was manipulating him to its heart's content, rewriting his plays, directing him through an appalling scenario of drunkenness, bravado and despair, and finally, with the memory of the said Dylan still in everyone's minds, demanding a death. Where the actual destruction of Dylan Thomas had been watched and welcomed with glee by only a comparatively small number of more or less literate bourgeois, for whom he was the necessary *poète maudit*, Brendan Behan's coarser and broader performance was entertainment for a multitude: he was the poor man's Dylan. I have said enough about the factors inherent in his own psychology which brought this situation about. Chief among the new precipitating elements must have been the knowledge that with his plays (all two of them) rewritten by other people and his books increasingly the products of 'collaboration', he was not in fact functioning as a creative artist at all, that the whole thing was to a large extent a tawdry fraud. Deaths of his kind are preceded by a death of the spirit. There is a sense in which he was the victim of society as clearly as if society had taken him out and shot him, but he was, one is forced to conclude, a willing victim, and Kavanagh's intuition of an inherent fraudulence in which there were elements of evil was, as far as one could see, from the outside at least, justified.

About a year after this encounter Robert Colquhoun and I were having a conversation during the course of which he asked: 'Was your grandfather ever an Irish seaman?'

I replied that so far as I knew he never had been.

'Would there be anything wrong with it if he was?' asked Robert.

'Not so far as I know,' I said. 'Personally I think it would be a very romantic avocation for him to have had. But why do you ask?'

'Well, the other day Robert and I met Brendan Behan for the first time, and he took us down to Mooneys of Cambridge Circus and he filled us full of drink, and the only thing he could say, and he kept on repeating it over and over again, was 'Cronin's fucking grandfather was an Irish seaman.'

'That's funny,' I said, but then it came to me. Between drink and Dublin and the inherent obscurity of the matter the purport of the charge had been lost on the Roberts. What Brendan had actually been saying was: 'Cronin's fucking grandfather was an R.I.C. man.'

After *Envoy* folded up, Kavanagh began a sporadic series of forays to London in search of the mythical city of converse, literary dignity and, of course, employment. His acquaintance was limited, as was his cash; his reputation almost non-existent; and there was the perennial problem of a base. Circumstance created psychological problems—where the taking of London is concerned confidence is a great factor—and so the early forays can only be described as a flop. Towards the end of the fifties, things improved. I wrote a piece in a fairly short-lived but not uninfluential magazine called *Nimbus* which made high claims and which attracted some attention. It was in response to this that I received one of the few letters I ever had from him: 'You never intrude, a sure sign of love', he wrote.

David Wright, one of the editors of the magazine, included him in *The Faber Book of Twentieth Century Verse*, as Mr. Costello and all the world were to be reminded during 'the trial'. Then quarterly review X came along, of which David and Patrick Swift were editors, while I was a member of the editorial board. X had a policy of pushing and publishing those whom it thought to be in one way or another neglected or overlooked: Hugh MacDiarmaid, Stevie Smith, Patrick Kavanagh among them, and X got around. A paperback firm, Ace Books, then run by my friend Frank Rudman, republished *Tarry Flynn*. Longmans, for whom the poet Thomas Blackburn was then acting as literary adviser, brought out a book, *Come Dance With Kitty Stobling*, mostly composed of the poems written during the new departure which had coincided with my sojourn on *The Bell*. He became for 1959 the mandatory Irish member of the trio who adjudicated on the Guinness awards for poetry, which meant that he had power, status and was put up in Brown's Hotel at the brewers' expense, about all of which more, as they say, hereafter. Then he found a hard-back firm, MacGibbon and Kee, who also reissued *Tarry Flynn*, eventually brought out his *Collected Poems* and backed him as a publisher should.

But the early years of the decade and the early forays were different. One in particular I remember as coinciding with one of my own sojourns in London, a rather depressing period and earlier in time, than the period of residence I have just been describing. He stayed with some friends, a youngish married couple, in Highgate. I was living in a doss-house and one Sunday when I came to visit him (at his invitation) we parted on rather bad terms because he affected to believe that I had ambitions to move in. I think it was my failure to steal a bottle of whisky from a hard-drinking Irish dentist who lived around the corner that precipitated his ill-humour. Paddy had been gleefully drinking with him throughout the morning. Then after a tiff he was ejected and had to face a more or less drinkless afternoon. The plan was as follows. Paddy wrote a note, allegedly of reconciliation, actually, to use the Irish word, *ráiméis*. I was to take it round to the dentist, ask to come in, give it to him, and say I had been told to wait for an answer. While he read it or answered it I was to lift a bottle of whisky from the sideboard (there would be more than one, I was told) hide it under my coat and bring it back.

Well, I failed. The dentist brought me in, gave me a drink and sat me down in front of the television, where he himself was sitting, still drinking; but whether because he was entranced by the programme or because he was past reading, he stuffed the note in his pocket without looking at it. I asked him a couple of times to read it, but he just waved me to silence and sat there, smiling at the set. Nor did he leave the room during the half hour or so that I was there. He may have been cuter than we thought.

Anyway, I failed, and we spent one of those long, drinkless, London Sunday afternoons that can almost cause a permanent darkening of the mind. Of the young couple he was staying with, the wife had been his friend before her marriage—the usual pattern. He was uneasy about overstaying his welcome all the same. 'To impose on people like this you'd want to be the centre of controversy,' he said. 'You know what I mean. There'd want to be a big row going on about you in print somewhere'. I did know what he meant, but when he went on to tell me about a review he had written for, I think, *The Tablet*, in which he had expressed violent and would-be controversial opinions about, I think, John Keats in the hope that there would be a row, the pathos became apparent.

One of the acquaintanceships he was trying to resume during this visit was that with John Betjeman. Betjeman had been in Dublin during the war years, when he had been press attaché at the British Embassy and had mixed a bit in the Pearl and elsewhere. He occurred in a poem of Paddy's, 'I Had a Future':

> 'Bring back the stretcher bed I slept in
> In a room in Drumcondra Road,
> Let John Betjeman call for me in a car.'

He was, according to Paddy now, 'a powerful fellow, a very powerful fellow in London', and of course he was building hopes of employment, further acquaintance and general literary advancement on a meeting or two. Unfortunately whenever he rang *Time and Tide* the girls would first ask who was speaking, request him to hold on and then come back to the phone to say that Mr. Betjeman was not available at the moment but could they take a message. After a few days of this Paddy gave up in despair and anger. He was getting, he said, 'the classical run-around' and he was naturally hurt in his pride as well as in his hopes. So, when, a little later, the poem was republished in a selection of Irish verse in the American publication *New World Writing*, Betjeman had been removed and the line read, 'Let Pat O'Connor call for me in a car.' When I went to work on the paper myself I learned the truth. Mr. Betjeman was a more than capable literary editor, but he saw no reason for daily attendance at the office. It was a breakdown in communications.

After a couple of years I left *Time and Tide* and went to live in a cottage in Sussex, resigned to me by a distinguished English contemporary who had no further emotional use for it. It was called Hearne Farm Cottage. It was beautiful, English and old, in fact the original peasant's hovel part of it was Elizabethan. It was on the edge of a wood, about a mile from the road, and except in the driest weather you could not bring the old Ford van that my poet friend had also bequeathed to me up the grass track which led to it. It had neither electricity nor running water. In winter-time it was necessary to wear Wellington boots whenever you went across the field and down the track to the van. At night you could hear stags, foxes and owls. In May and June the whole valley rang with the sweet-throated song of the nightingale. There were, literally, roses round the door.

It was to Hearne that Kavanagh came, riding down with us after one of our visits to London along the Portsmouth Road in the old Ford van and rejoicing in the English names of the places we passed, repeating 'The Hog's Back' over to himself with deep satisfaction.

He declared at once that country living brought back earlier memories and he was delighted by country circumstances–peeing outside the door at night under the stars, the oil lamps, the wood fire, the walk up the lane. 'Did ye bring in the bike?', 'Did ye shut the door of the hen-house?' he would enquire ironically in the evenings.

We had been up in town for a few days; it was the end of the month; and there were several cheques for me in the postbox at the end of the lane when we arrived, the reward of a month's reviewing and the other forms of hack-writing by which I lived. Unfortunately their presence gave Paddy the idea–or at least he affected to believe–that a similar amount of money arrived by almost every post. He therefore saw no reason to abate his drinking to the modest country level of a few bitters every now and then that I had had to adopt for survival purposes, nor, probably, could he have endured such abatement anyway. Since he had no money himself this led to some strain. Every afternoon and again each evening after supper he would expect to be taken to one or other of the pubs in Haslemere or in the villages round about, and in the pubs he would drink only whiskey. At closing time a bottle–or at the very least a half-bottle– would have to be taken back to the cottage. After a few days of this, during which the money, which of course had to last for the whole of the coming month, vanished rapidly, he had the face to assert: 'It was the best thing I ever did comin' down here for the cure. It's very, very painful, but sure if I survive it, it'll make a man of me.' Late one night by the fireside, when such drink as had been brought back had been consumed, there were words about something or other. After a few exchanges he brought the matter to a good-humoured end by declaring mournfully: 'If we only had another bottle of whiskey now we'd have time for several rows and reconciliations.'

He was subject to panics in the middle of the night and the cottage was lit only by oil lamps, among them two somewhat complicated vaporising affairs that I had bought when some time before I had been in receipt of an exceedingly welcome grant from the Royal Literary Fund. When Paddy heard noises or whatever he heard in the night he

169

would immediately attempt to procure himself a steady light, but he could not manage any of the lamps, even the simple ones, and replace globes though I did, the rate of attrition was terrible. We could hear him blundering about in the dark downstairs in the living-room where he slept, repeating 'Oh dear, oh dear' to himself, and overturning and smashing objects of all descriptions, including lamps. At length he did something to the stem of one of the vaporising lamps, through which the oil came up under pressure, so that it never lit properly again. He declared that what he needed was a nightcap, which puzzled me for a moment. I knew he did not mean the article of headgear, but he always had a drink of some sort right up to bedtime. Then I discovered that he meant a small bottle of whiskey from which he could drink in the middle of the night when thoughts or illusions or despairs got the better of him. This was regularly procured thereafter, but of course it was as regularly drunk when all else ran out, so the panics and the consequent blunderings about in the darkness of the night continued unabated.

I had also bought with the bountiful grant a small portable radio. This had a device to ensure that you could not close the lid of the case while the radio remained on and thus waste the battery: if you did so it would emit a high-pitched buzz. One afternoon while Thérèse and I were out, Paddy closed the lid of the box, with needless to say, the radio on, and the thing began to make its helpful noise. Utterly baffled by the reason for this and unable to do anything about it, he had got into a state and started to bang it on the table. This of course effectually silenced it. It was while listening to a commentary on the Grand National on this radio two days previously that he had broken the glass in the back door. On the second circuit only one Irish runner remained standing and as he fell further back Paddy, who was sitting outside on a barrel in the April sunshine, began to get more and more delighted, hugging himself and shaking his enormous shoulders from side to side with glee while he crowed, 'The Irish are bolloxed, the Irish are bolloxed', until eventually, after one especially violent paroxysm, his shoulder went through the glass.

It was no wonder, then, that when he went through the floor of the van, he felt that he had to offer some sort of explanation. The van was an old war-time utility model and the floors were made of plywood. One afternoon, as we set out for the village, Paddy sat in beside me with such violence that wood under the passenger seat on his side gave way with a tearing sound and the earth of the lane became visible underneath. He got out with some reluctance while I put a couple of boards across between the driveshaft casing and the frame on the door side. Then, 'It's the destructive power of the poet,' he said. 'My father told me, "You broke everything on the farm except the crowbar. And you bent that."'

He enjoyed aspects of English country life immensely, however. Talking to yokels in the pubs, 'the great submerged' as he called them, particularly pleased him, though he understood little of what they said. He was delighted to be told that ten men were kept constantly at work repairing the miles-long wall of the nearby Petworth estate, like the men who paint the Forth Bridge. He commented on the woodlands and the great oaks that grew beside the country roads, evidence of England's wealth compared to treeless Ireland. He asked a little boy, the son of one of the cottagers at the end of the lane, what his religion was. 'Well, we used to be C. of E. but me and me sister didn't get invited to the Sunday school outing, they thought we wasn't good enough, see, so mother said we'd pack it', the little boy replied, which rejoiced Kavanagh so much that 'mother said we'd pack it' became one of his phrases about religion thereafter.

He was delighted to learn that Lord Tennyson had owned the large and rather gloomy house called Aldworth on the top of nearby Blackdown and that when the old poet, something of a radical in his youth, had acceded to Gladstone's request and taken that unfortunate peerage, he had called himself Baron Tennyson of Freshwater and Aldworth. Of course he pretended to be more interested in the possibility that the Tennyson who captained England at cricket had lived there. He would gaze up at Blackdown reverentially as we went down the field outside the house and say, 'Do you tell me that Tennyson lived up there?' I would assent to this and Paddy would slowly repeat, in tones of wonder, 'Well, Well. Do you mind that now. Tennyson. The great batsman. That captained England.'

He was also very pleased when I took him up the side of the slope on which we lived and showed him the great stretch of the Sussex weald rolling away into the blue beneath us. Of course he knew about the Weald, as I did myself, from Belloc and Kipling, but when I told him that it had been abandoned for centuries to woods and charcoal burners because of its stiff rich soil that not even the Romans could plough, he repeated over and over, 'Not even the Romans could plough it. Not even the Romans.' There was to him, the ploughman, something magical about the age of the craft.

He was pleased with his visit, even to the extent of accompanying me up to London and coming back down with me again. There was only one flaw. The time when he was to lecture again was coming up and he was barren of ideas. He had lectured the previous year to packed audiences of cheering students, delivering himself apparently of dogmatisms, dismissals and occasional profundities, having in fact the sort of ostensible success among the seemingly sympathetic and irreverent young that in his weaker moments he had dreamed of. Now the time had come round again and he had nothing new to say.

I told him, I am afraid, not to bother, that the people who gave him the money would be just as pleased if he kept away from the place and never lectured again. This did not please him at all. He spoke of his duty, to young people, to his friends, 'to all the friends I never knew I had', but the fact of the matter was that he had tasted the heady brew of popular acclaim and he had no intention of giving it up.

The difficulty now was, however, that he had nothing to say, or at least 'if I have anything to say I don't know what it is.' There were many books in the house and he took to ravening through these, scattering them behind him as he went. 'I'm looking for something that might spark me', he said. He was particularly fond of aphorisms—indeed he was an aphorist himself—and he searched through a selection of Hoffmansthal's aphorisms with growing excitement, until at length he found it was 'empty'—a not uncommon experience where that particular form is concerned.

On British Railways (in those days at least) Scotch was served in miniature bottles enclosed in a cardboard box. When I saw Paddy off he sat into the dining-car, just opposite where I stood on the platform. The train only stopped in Haslemere for about sixty seconds, but before it moved out he had managed to obtain two little cardboard boxes. I don't think he did lecture that year, nor, so far as I know, did he ever lecture again.

All good things come to an end, they say; and as the beautiful, prolonged summer of 1959 waned to its October close we left Hearne and returned to London. It seemed, on the whole, easier to survive there. We took an empty flat upstairs from the Irish poet Leland Bardwell in a gaunt house in Holloway which was under sentence of death. Leland was the most hospitable of women and her floors were strewn with mattresses on which various figures lay sleeping or meditating at all hours of the day and night. Her part of the house was, you might say, the seacoast of bohemia.

The local was the Holloway Castle, which is anchored under the lee of Her Majesty's prison. Thither one night arrived Robert MacBryde, announcing, 'I have burnt my lover. I have burned the house with my lover in it.'

The Roberts had been living in the country too, and in fact MacBryde had found a gallery and had been working for an exhibition. Colquhoun had had a full retrospective exhibition in the Whitechapel Gallery shortly before we went to Hearne. He had done a lot of new work for it and that he was able to work at all, in terms of either spirit or circumstance, had been remarkable; yet the results, in terms of either sales or reputation, had not been what he had some right to expect. Still the move to the country had been at least a regenerative one, and now that MacBryde had been working again and had a show in prospect they were at least not giving up as before. So what was all this about burning the house, his lover and, presumably, the paintings? It appeared that there had been a tiff. It also appeared that

MacBryde had done something drunkenly inconclusive by way of attempting to destroy his own paintings by fire while Colquhoun lay sleeping, the method adopted being to pile oiled rags safely against the outside of the studio wall and throw a match amongst them. Then he had made for the train. It further appeared that debts had been mounting in the village, the butcher and the pub in particular being owed colossal sums; that between work and worry the strain had steadily increased; and that sufficient paintings now existed, or had until recently existed, for the exhibition. It appeared to me at least that both lover and paintings were unburned; that it was only a matter of time before the former arrived also; and that the main problem would be to get the paintings up to London as well. MacBryde had in fact simply decided to bring things to an end down there and he had behaved according to the well-known adage that the way to do this is to bring things to an end.

In fact it was all of two days before Colquhoun showed up, but he was quite unburned; and by a miracle of organisation he had succeeded in getting the paintings, which were of course also unburned, on the train along with him. With the paintings now safely at the gallery, the exhibition coming up and the country butcher and publican at a distance, the Roberts settled snugly into Leland's also. The technique of sudden and absolute abandonment, so widely practised amongst us all, had been put into effect once more.

Was it at this time that the attempt was made to murder Kavanagh? I cannot remember whether it was at the beginning of the visit he was now to pay to London or immediately prior to his visit to Hearne that I first heard the story from his own lips. I was standing at the corner of Dean Street and Old Compton Street on what must have been a summer, or at least a warm spring evening–for I remember that we none of us were wearing overcoats and that we had for some reason been standing there for quite some time–talking to the poet David Wright and a distinguished French critic and man of letters to whom David had just introduced me. Now my friend David Wright is stone-deaf and the Frenchman, although a well-known translator of the works of Shakespeare into *la langue Française*, did not appear to have much English, if in fact he had any at all. The conversation therefore presented some difficulties, and I was just about to suggest our removal to a public house, where at least the better light would allow David to lip-read and the general noise and hubbub might relieve the embarrassment both of the *homme des lettres* and myself (the reader will already be aware that my own French is minimal) when I heard my name being called in accents well known to me.

I turned from my companions and, lo and behold, who should I see hastening towards us from the general direction of Shaftesbury Avenue but the aforementioned Irish poet Patrick Kavanagh. He was evidently in a high state of excitement, not to say agitation, and his first words were, 'They tried to murder me. They tried to do away with me.' There followed a vivid, albeit somewhat confused, tale of a dastardly attempt on his life which had taken place a few days before in Dublin. It appeared that he had been drinking in a hostelry in Haddington Road, which was a favourite haunt of his, with some companions. Although constant associates, these, he now wished to make clear, could hardly be described as intellectual or social equals, and in fact the words he was now applying to them might lead one to the belief that he had known all along that they were of a criminal disposition, and engaged in the pettiest and lowest forms of criminality at that. In fact I knew the place and I was acquainted with some of the gentlemen described. On this particular occasion, having apparently planned his death with some foresight, they put a drug of sorts, what he called 'a Mickey Finn', into his drink. Feeling the effects of this, though not rendered unconscious by it, he left the public house and began, with difficulty, to make his way home. For some reason which his present narrative did not make clear he apparently crossed the road and attempted to make his way along the canal bank, a perilous place at the best of times, the more so in the dark and dead of night. Suddenly through drug-benumbed senses he heard footsteps behind him and voices which he recognised as those of his erstwhile drinking companions. Sensing danger, he attempted to run but the rough uneven ground as well as the effects of the drug impeded him and a moment later he was seized and flung bodily into the canal. As the water closed over him, he heard a voice which he recognised full well say, 'That's the end of him, the old bollocks.'

His feelings at that moment may be imagined, but indeed, in this respect at least, the description he now gave me and my uncomprehending friends left little to the imagination. 'It was rage,' he said, 'enabled me to survive.' And so, though no swimmer, he somehow got to the opposite bank, climbed out and made his way to the nearby flat of a woman friend of his. She ministered to him and put him to bed, and the following day, when he was a little recovered from the effects of his terrible experience she bought him an entire new outfit of clothes to replace that which had been utterly ruined by immersion in the canal. This accounted for his well-turned-out, not to say fashionable, appearance at the moment.

Harrowing though Mr. Kavanagh's experience may well be thought to be, the reader might here spare a thought for my own distress as I attempted to relay to my deaf friend and our French acquaintance the fact that an attempt had just been made on this distinguished Irish poet's life and to keep them (if I may hazard a French phrase) *au fait* with his narrative in all its strange turns and bewildering complexity of detail. This might not have been necessary except that Mr. Kavanagh insisted on addressing his story to them as well as to myself and they were naturally constrained to enquire from me from time to time (and the whole story took a long time) what he was saying now.

But enough of that. Was there a grain of truth in it? Certainly Paddy clung to the story for many years and he even wrote an article called 'The Man They Could Not Kill' for the *Irish Digest* about it. It became in fact one of his prime myths.

Strangely though, he appeared to remain on excellent terms with the man who was supposed to be the instigator of the attempt. When I returned to Dublin from Spain some years later I found them to be daily intimates, as they had been before. I had, I am afraid, the temerity to remark on the oddity, to say the least, of this association between the putative murderer and the murderee. 'It's a very erotic relationship,' was Kavanagh's reply.

One other remark may throw some light on the affair. I met by chance another of the alleged would-be homicides and I (jocularly) questioned him about it. 'I didn't throw Kavanagh into any canal, but I'll tell you this much—the man I'd like to get my hands on is the fellow that pulled the ould bollocks out,' was the reply.

Anyway, whether it was on this visit or a previous one that I first heard the sensational story of the murder attempt, Kavanagh now came to stay in Holloway also. Leland's was the first roof he shared with Robert MacBryde. It was not to be the last.

His attitude to the Roberts was ambivalent, and illustrative of something rather strange in his general attitude to London acquaintances. At home Paddy was intolerant, but democratic enough, associating daily with all sorts of people who had no claim to intellectual or artistic distinction. In London, unless through circumstance and for the sake of circumstance, he desired to associate only with those who had some claim to fame. The object of the London forays, the myth that lay behind them, was that he would find his proper company and his proper ambience there. But there were gaps in his education and in his general knowledge, particularly outside literature, which led him into mistakes, one way or the other. When he met the Roberts first he remained unaware for some time that they had, or ever had had, any reputation as painters and he gave them, to some extent, the cold shoulder. 'The little fellow is the most amusing,' he said reluctantly one day. Latterly he had become aware of the fact that, certain appearances to the contrary, they 'belonged' somewhere in the dream that was London and England and his attitude had changed. Similarly when he met Julian MacLaren-Ross first he said afterwards, 'That fellow's a frightful bore' (he was) but he had not heard the name. When I mentioned it again it rang a bell and the next day, when Julian came into the French pub, Paddy said eagerly: 'I say, are you the man who wrote *Bitten By The Tarantula?*' It was of course a form of recognition from one artist to another, but there was more to it than that; and, in keeping with the dream, mediocre poets and writers, whose equivalents at home would have been lashed from his company with whips and scorpions, or at the least dismissed, satirised and denigrated behind their backs, were said to have, in conversation at least, 'the authentic thing, the true Parnassian note.'

Now, because they were all pigging in together, his relationship with the Roberts became more human, but I do believe he was comforted still by the thought that he was not entirely wasting his time in London when he went down to the Holloway Castle or the Prince Edward with them for a few bitters.

Paddy slept on an actual bed which Leland had specially set up for him in the living-room. He was usually back home and tucked up there before other people began to arrive, but as they did, he would begin to wake up and take some interest in the proceedings. He had recently been to America as the guest of a woman friend and he was wearing American underpants which for some reason were decorated with large red hearts. Sometimes, if the Roberts or someone else had brought drink back and the proceedings were really to his liking, he would raise himself on one elbow, or even sit up in bed in his decorative underwear and join in the chat. If he was fully awake and enjoying himself he might even sing. Nowadays he always contrived to have a naggin or a half-bottle beneath his pillow for consumption in the watches of the night, and he would take the odd slug from this every now and then, though woe betide anybody who asked him for a drop.

His principal topics of conversation at this time were America and Kraft-Ebbing. He had recently returned from the one and it appeared he had recently been reading some sort of edition of the other. He regarded both with a strange mixture of naïvety and sophistication. What appeared to have struck him most in America was the Automat (a sort of old-fashioned, self-service café, really dating from the O. Henry era) round the corner from the hotel where he stayed; analogously, in the case of Kraft-Ebbing, quite unremarkable manifestations of sexuality appeared to fill him with wonder, while others more *outré* apparently seemed to him to be commonplace. On the occasions when he decided he wanted company he seemed to be very pleased with the Roberts' reminiscences of Ayrshire and, no mean singer himself, he enjoyed hearing MacBryde sing when the latter was reasonably sober.

He had discovered that whiskey was considerably cheaper in the off-licences than it was by the measure in the pubs, and in the pubs he affected to drink bitter. In fact he would have a flask bottle of whiskey in his jacket pocket and conversation with him in the pub was always punctuated by his frequent visits to the jakes for the more efficacious form of refreshment. He fondly imagined that one was unaware of the purpose of these visits and, as they multiplied, he would sing the praises of the beer. 'Not bad stuff at all, not bad stuff at all, this bitter', he would say. 'It sets up a buzz. It sets up a faint buzz.'

One day everybody was late arising and coming on to three o'clock there was something approaching panic about getting to the pub, which was a good ten minutes' walk away. I still had the van and everybody piled into it, the Roberts and a peripatetic Irishman who was staying upstairs with us into the back; Paddy, needless to say, into the front, beside me. Because time was so short I accelerated violently as we took off. The back doors, which were always difficult to fasten, flew open, and the Irishman, who had been partly leaning against them, fell out. He put down his hands to break his fall but unfortunately his foot had got caught on something inside, and for a moment or two he was dragged. He began to shout and, although I could not see what was wrong, I stamped on the brakes. At this moment Kavanagh said angrily: 'Drive on out of that. He's only looking for attention.' Getting to the pub was of course the most important matter.

Also resident in Leland's at this time was my friend, Anthony Carson, the news of whose death has reached me only now as I write. On most days the Roberts, Kavanagh and Carson would make their joint or separate ways into Soho. If one was at home for the evening in the flat upstairs one would sooner or later hear the three separate returnings, Paddy of course being first back and the Roberts usually last. There would be the faint sound of brakes, the unmistakable throb of a London taxi engine while money was searched for, change was counted and pleasantries or sometimes, alas, words of abuse were exchanged with the driver. Then one would hear the faint ping as the flag was raised again and the noise of the receding taxi was replaced by fumblings at the front door, accompanied in Paddy's case usually by groans or self-commiserations, in the Roberts' all too often by the rise and fall of argument. Whenever in London nowadays I hear a late taxi stop in the street to discharge a fare, it brings those summer nights back.

When Paddy became a judge of the Guinness awards he was put up during the necessary visits to London in Brown's Hotel. Brown's is, of course, or was then, the resort of the landed gentry on their visits to London. He was not happy there. He was afraid to ring room service at night because in America, he insisted, the night porters always sent you up a woman, and he didn't want that. Nothing would convince him that Brown's was different. At length he took to ordering himself a cold chicken and a bottle of whiskey in the mornings and bringing them round to his friends' places of abode. If suitably accompanied in a taxi he might sometimes return in the afternoon and go up to his room long enough to order another bottle of whiskey. This was the extent of his residence there. And yet, strange mixture that he was, he had a very accurate sense of what luxury hotels that had any tradition were all about. Once, some time before, we had met a wealthy young man, whose mother Paddy knew, in the French pub.

'How's your mother?' he enquired.

'She's in Claridge's at the moment,' the young man replied. 'She's going into a nursing home.'

'What does she want to do that for? Sure Claridge's is a kind of a nursing home itself,' said Paddy.

It was while he was a judge of the Guinness awards that I discovered something about him I had not known before. If he did you an underhand bad turn he would react violently by imagining that you had wronged him in all sorts of mysterious ways. Many people have this characteristic; indeed it belongs to human nature; but Paddy had an exceptional ability to forget his own behaviour and concentrate on imagined grievances. Very likely this was because at heart he was not really treacherous and thus, when he behaved treacherously, he was subconsciously very deeply disturbed.

With the dawn of a new decade we went to live in Spain and, after much migration through the islands and elsewhere, we fetched up in an Andalusian farmhouse. This was outside a pueblo called Alhaurin El Grande, on the road between Malaga and Ronda. Alhaurin is a corruption of the Moorish, and it means 'the garden of God'. Well watered and intricately irrigated, the land around Alhaurin was indeed, compared to much of the neighbouring countryside, favoured by the Gods. All the good fruits of the earth grew there; figs, oranges, lemons, pomegranates, grapes, olives, onions, garlic and maize. The people of the pueblo, though not rich, were by no means as poor as Andalusian peasants can be, and they owned their own land. The farmers all lived in the pueblo itself, which was arranged cubistically, round a hill surmounted by a church. Every morning at the same hour they rode out in endless single file, each man sitting sideways on his mule and controlling it with a single rein attached to the bridle, and every evening with the end of the light they rode back, silently, in single file. The mules were brought into the houses by the front door and appeared to be stabled inside; actually they were kept in yards at the back.

Our house was known as the Huertos Altos, to distinguish it from the Huertos Abajos, the only other farmhouse in the locality, which was at the bottom of the hill on the other side of the town. It was airy, commodious and, like all Andalusian houses, built to keep out the heat; this made it cold when the weather was cold. Its disadvantage was a piggery next door which brought flies and in the hot weather seemed to increase the general oppressiveness.

It was here that we learned of the death of Robert Colquhoun, by means of a letter from Katherine Moloney, a mutual friend who was to marry Patrick Kavanagh about five years later. It seemed that a new small gallery in Bloomsbury had offered him an exhibition; he had been working hard, sometimes late at night; and one night he had collapsed and died. MacBryde had been in the adjoining room, sleeping; he had heard a 'terrible shout' and had reached Robert in time to hold him in his arms while he died. So, did he die of work, or drink, or not eating, or plain heart disease, or a combination of them all? Apart from the fact that the Roberts for long periods did not eat enough anyway, Colquhoun was a most reluctant eater when he was drinking and would even occasionally sweep dishes that had been ordered for him in restaurants off the table. He was forty-seven. At least he was working when he died.

I wrote to Robert MacBryde immediately, saying that he would know best what he wanted to do himself, but that if he wanted to get away for a while and could manage it, he was more than welcome to come to us. Not long afterwards came a night of storm and rain of an intensity unusual at that time of year. My Spanish friends were sometimes in the habit of calling late at night in search of drink or converse—it is not done for an Andalusian peasant to sit late over the wine in his own house—so, when I heard a repeated knocking on the big double front door, it was with some reluctance that I opened the bedroom shutter and called out through the window, *'Quien es? Que pasa?'*

From down below in the rain and darkness came a voice; 'It's me. It's Robert'. And so it was. Apparently Francis Bacon had given him the money to go abroad for a while and he had crossed the channel and driven all the way to Southern Spain with the Scots dancer, John MacDonald. He had a bottle of Scotch and we sat up to drink it. Unfortunately the only other thing I had to drink in the house was a bottle of 'corriente', 'running' anis, the cheap, unbranded kind that is sold on draft, out of the barrel. We drank that too, and the following day I was ill, hearing voices, Colquhoun's among them. The doctor came, and after him the *practicante,* that peculiar Spanish institution, neither nurse, student nor apprentice doctor, whose job it is to give injections, usually with a rusty needle.

I stayed in bed for two or three days, drinking lemon juice made from fruit just off the tree. News travels fast in that part of the world and my Spanish friends came to visit me in large numbers.

'They are coming from all quarters', said MacBryde helpfully, 'to see their dying king.'

He was at that moment rather in love with death and his inexorable notions of chieftainship and the clan system, always associated with Colquhoun, were for the moment transferred to Spain.

Meanwhile he was becoming quite a figure in the pueblo himself and establishing a pattern of behaviour which he was to maintain with intervals for some weeks. For most of this time he refused to draw a sober breath. Alone or accompanied he would be in the cafés until the last one shut, about two o'clock in the morning. Even then he could not sleep and one would hear him pottering about in the night, until eventually, almost at first light, he would be off to the cafés again, the market café, being the first to open, usually being the first he would visit. Though he never learned one solitary word of the language, not even how to count, he established an instant *rapport* with the locals, singing his songs, doing his dances and listening with a happy smile of understanding while they talked to him—as many primitive people will do, it being apparently beyond their comprehension that others should not understand their language, which even children can speak. Robert's drinking in the local cafés was punctuated by visits to Malaga or Torremolinos with John or myself. He appeared to have lots of money and he would refuse nobody; bootblack, beggar, lottery ticket seller—indeed the lottery tickets he bought and lost were of huge denominations and it is possible that some of the myriads became worth considerable sums. It was obvious that he was in a state of shock and a really heavy bout of unrestrained drinking may well have been the best thing for him. Apart from the ritual bouts of obsessional anger with Colquhoun he had never really suffered serious transformations of personality in drink. His speech remained the same, though his conversation became more repetitive and more gnomic. He danced and sang, but I never saw him insensible, or incapable of loco-motion. So, even now, he was not difficult to bear with. I brought him to visit Gerald Brenan and his charming wife who lived in the neighbouring village of Alhaurin Del Torre and, though he was exceedingly drunk, he was so capable of comporting himself that Gerald was surprised afterwards when I said something about the state he was in. Yet there had been a change in him and it was more marked in drink than otherwise. Always loquacious, he was now positively garrulous. A constant stream of reminiscence and anecdote flowed from him, much of it to do with Colquhoun, all of whose failings, in so far as they had ever been counted, were now forgotten. Oddly enough there was a good deal of wisdom mixed up in all this, life-wisdom which would emerge often when least expected. In a funny way Robert made more sense than he used to do before; and this although he was now quite definitely becoming subject to delusions. They were gentle, beneficent delusions, not at all like those that were to be so apparent in Kavanagh when next I saw him, but they were delusions all the same.

It was, I suppose, inevitable that MacBryde should gravitate to Ireland in the end. His celticism, always present in his psychology, had been, if anything, growing since Colquhoun's death. One had always heard a lot about the Irish side of his ancestry, though what one heard was not very coherent, for the MacBrydes were sometimes said to have been itinerant Irish tinkers, sometimes 'tatie howkers' who had settled in Ayrshire. Now the improbabilities increased, but he was at least more specific. He was, it seemed, related to Major John MacBride, Maud Gonne's husband and one of the transfigured martyrs of Yeats's poem, who had been executed in Easter Week; indeed there was said to be a picture of the Major hanging in the house at home in Maybole; for all the MacBrydes were very proud of him and the degree of cousinhood was sometimes explicated in bewildering detail. His anti-Englishness, always a feature of his psychology too, was now bound up with the treatment that the art world in particular and the English in general had meted out to his friend, and through a valid extension of feeling Colquhoun was transformed vaguely but nonetheless poetically into a chieftain of the Gael betrayed by the Sassenach.

Nor was he happy in London, where I next saw him. Colquhoun's death had made it a desolate city for him. Many of his other friends, Dylan Thomas and John Minton among them, had died in recent years. All our circle was breaking up, as circles will, and the licensing laws had even been changed so that the old Caves de France, the Roberts' afternoon refuge for so long, was closed. For a time he occupied a little room off the landing in Elizabeth Smart's flat in Bayswater. He would apparently come home early there, go to bed and read Dickens. Sebastian Barker, Elizabeth's son, would often hear him weeping quietly to himself as he passed the door.

Then he made the acquaintance of an Irish doctor friend of mine in London; they became friends; for a while they shared a flat; and this put Ireland more than ever in Robert's mind. Consequently when Louis MacNeice's widow, who had a restaurant in Kinsale, Co. Cork, conceived the idea of running a summer school of painting there and wanted a painter of some note to oversee the aspirations of the guests, Robert leaped at the chance. His sojourn there was not, however, a success. He had no money, but he was drinking heavily. He stole wine from the restaurant and drank it in an outhouse under pretext of communing with the hens. In the condition he was in he was not suited to encourage Sunday painters to express their conception of reality. When I met him in O'Dwyers of Lower Leeson Street one evening he had fled from Kinsale under a cloud, apparently having taken somebody's handbag from a motor-car and spent whatever was in it on drink.

We had left Spain after I had finished a book there some time before. London seemed dead and depressing to me also. Soho was a wilderness of strip clubs and pornographic book-shops. The drinking clubs were shut. My friends were dead or had gone to live in the country or abroad. I had little intention of resuming the life of reviewer and general literary odd-job-man. And for the first time in years I was full of a strange yearning for my own country. Besides which, it seemed impossible to find any place to live in London; and if I wanted to write another book on the money I had got, Dublin was still cheaper.

Nevertheless it was probably a mistake to return there at that juncture. There were elements in the situation to suggest that I was in fact kicking the ball away from my own feet for the hundredth time. However, life is full of mistakes; and one can only hope that they do turn out in retrospect to be truly 'volitional and the portals of discovery'.

One of the things that shocked and depressed me in Dublin was Kavanagh's condition. He was now thoroughly far gone in whiskey and for the most part he sat in McDaid's leaning forward with his head sunk, clutching his stomach, taking little or no part in the conversation around him. He had always been hypochondriac and had always complained of stomach trouble, eating quantities of bicarbonate out of the palm of his hand and leaving a trail of it behind him wherever he went. One morning years ago I had come into the pub to find him sitting in front of a table on which reposed his packet of bread soda, a glass of ginger wine and a little jar of actual ground ginger. It appeared that the bread soda was necessary to him because of his acid stomach, but too much bread soda dried up the acid altogether and that was dangerous. Ginger restored the acid and he now proceeded to shake some ground ginger into his glass of ginger wine and drink the mixture. After this he felt the need for a drink. He was off the whiskey and so he decided to order himself a glass of port. At that time he was having a long flirtation with port as a substitute for whiskey. When asked by barmen if he preferred any particular vintage or variety he was accustomed to reply impatiently 'Port. Port. Just port. Any port in a storm.' However, on this particular morning the port did not suffice, and so it, and the ginger, and the ginger wine, and the bread soda were succeeded by several large brandies.

Now, however, he appeared to be genuinely sick and would sit for long periods in a silence broken only by occasional hawkings, groans and 'oh dears', apparently listening to the chat but seldom intervening. There was a big efflux of young poets in Dublin at that time; indeed because of the boom conditions then prevailing and the libertarian attitudes created by the Second Vatican Council there was a big efflux of everything; homo- and heterosexuality, folk-song, drink and culture. Kavanagh was therefore well surrounded and he did not go short of acclaim. To many of those who surrounded him he was a comparatively new phenomenon and they were pleased to be in his company even though he did little but hawk and clutch himself and mutter. His *Collected Poems* were shortly to come out; when he wrote anything he gave it to the little magazines—of which there were two or three edited from McDaid's—for immediate cash, and so his prestige among the young was high. He had achieved the long sought for position of Ard Fhile, without sacrificing the loyalty of what passed for the *avant-garde*.

And yet if he did not go short of adulation, there must have been other things he missed. With perhaps one exception there was nobody in his immediate circle who displayed any acerbity or independence of judgment at all. He had always been happy to feed a bit on certain individuals' enthusiasms and judgments; you never knew when a chance remark might not enliven him. Like others of his stature too, although he preferred non-literary conversation, he needed the support derived from a tacit acknowledgment of the supreme importance of the activity to which he had, after all, devoted his life, an acknowledgment to be revealed perhaps only occasionally and obliquely and through a half-hint of the blade; but what he heard around him in McDaid's now was for the most part indiscriminate poetic enthusiasm, and it must have nearly choked him.

Yet there was an evident sense in which he had made his bed and was happy enough to lie on it. It seemed that now he preferred to associate with people of little judgment, and a man has always his own reasons for doing that, be they good or bad.

He had, it is true, a few old friends who were outside the McDaid's circle altogether, his alleged would-be murderer among them, but his relationship with them was relaxed and non-literary, except in so far as he chose to air his own views on this or that. The truth is that at the end he had no serious fellow-artist, or, to put it another way, where poetry was concerned, no fellow-spirit, with whom he had any sort of association at all.

This book, as at the risk of wearying the reader, I must even now repeat, has not been about myself; nor, except incidentally and as a matter falling most particularly within my observation, has it been about the relationship of others with myself. Therefore suffice it to say that my relationship with Kavanagh, in so far as it continued to exist, was not, at the end, a happy one. Since a certain point, in fact I think since he had come to be, in however tenuous a way, a little in one's debt for publication or the advancement of his reputation and since one had begun to publish on any sort of scale oneself, there had been a falling-off, a process sporadic-ally checked and even reversed by mutual association and consent, but complicated and accelerated now by others' willingness to carry tales, report remarks and generally fish for whatever they could in troubled waters.

And there were comic factors exacerbating all this. Shortly after my return to Dublin I had published a satirical novel which contained portraits of several people that we jointly knew and which achieved some local *réclame*. In some obscure way he seemed to feel that he should have written this; and it was but a short step from there to feeling that I had stolen some sort of a march on him by doing so. Further, within a year or so after my return to Dublin there was a small spate of anthologies in which he was heavily represen-ted but in which I was represented as well, we being the only two local poets who were. In the normal course of events he would have brought these, however casually, into McDaid's and, however offhandedly, accepted whatever sort of kudos were going. Now he could not do so without serving some-one else's parochial reputation and elevating him to some-thing suspiciously like equality at the same time, and his pleasure was to that extent spoiled.

But to pass judgment on this kind of thing, even if one felt the need or was inclined to, would be wrong. P. K. was now, to a very great extent, a caricature of himself. He was drinking whiskey with wild abandon and in large measures all the time. 'Throw a ball of malt into me,' was his prelimin-ary injunction to a barman. And in order to sleep he was tak-ing barbiturates recklessly and at ill-judged intervals through the night. 'Sleeping-sweets' he called them. The effect was not calculated to keep him in any very stern contact with reality.

Some time after Robert MacBryde's flight from Cork our

doctor friend took a largish flat in Upper Leeson Street. Here MacBryde went to stay and here, by a natural gravitational process, went Kavanagh as well. The famous flat in Pembroke Road had long been abandoned and latterly he had spent some time in the basement flat that Leland had taken in the lower part of Leeson Street, lying on a sofa beside the window in the cluttered living-room and asking her to make 'Complan' for him at all hours of the day and night, for he was at the time on a 'Complan' jag. Then he had taken a room from an eccentric old lady that Leland knew in Lower Mount Street. When my friend Peter Cohen, author of *The Diary of a Simple Man,* took the room some time later he found a peculiar white powder scattered in drifts over the floor. At first he thought it was some sort of insecticide, liberally distributed—or something even more sinister. It turned out to be bicarbonate of soda, a relic of Kavanagh's occupation.

Now, however, both he and MacBryde were happily ensconced in Upper Leeson Street. The flat was not very luxurious, but it was big enough for Kavanagh to have a little room to himself at the top of the ultimate small flight of stairs. This looked over the street and here at all hours you could see the electric light burning. He said he could not sleep now without a light, but it is probable that in the true sense he hardly slept at all. The bottle to keep under the pillow was now an absolute necessity and he would actually drink from it without appearing to wake up, as a baby does, the difference being that Kavanagh had to unscrew the top and replace it again as well as putting the bottle to his lips and imbibing. This he would do without spilling a drop and without opening his eyes.

Shortly after they had taken up residence there they were joined by another lodger or guest, a retired country schoolmaster who drank in McDaid's and whom we all knew, a man of some culture in an old-fashioned way, and, I think it is true to say, of an equally eccentric disposition. They made, within the limits of their circumstances, an almost contented-seeming trio, all, in their various ways, past it, whatever it was; all with little routines which brought some sort of solace and filled out the day.

Robert had taken to Ireland like a duck to water and he was happy that in this *ménage* he was allowed to do the housekeeping and that there was housekeeping to do. Thus, first thing in the morning, he would do some cleaning up. Then he would light the fire and make coffee. Kavanagh would now have arisen and would be sitting in his shirt sleeves and braces finishing off whatever whiskey was left in his night bottle. If Robert and the schoolmaster were lucky there would be a small distribution. The ration was an egg-cupful and if either of them were especially in favour and the mood was right he might get two.

After this, and after their various ablutions had been made, they would all three go to the pub around the corner, the Sussex House, together. The time spent here depended on various factors, the time of rising and the amount of money Kavanagh judged the other two to have among them. In the forenoons in the Sussex House he was most like his old self, interested, opinionated, dogmatic and humorous, but sooner or later he would go off to McDaid's and almost inevitably go into a long period of decline, broken perhaps by an afternoon nap or visits to the bookmakers. Robert would now do some shopping and put on a stew or a *pot au feu* of some kind. He would leave this over a low gas and go off to McDaid's himself, not to return until closing time. By then of course the fire and the gas would be out and the stew would be spoiled but this did not matter. The domestic gods had been honoured. Robert had absolutely no cash at all and no source of income beyond what our doctor friend gave him. There would be no strain about accepting this and there would be talk of pictures to be sold or having been sold to one person or another in London, and suggestions that money might be about to accrue, but all this was, and was understood to be, more necessary to his dignity than anything else. Once in McDaid's he rarely went short of drink and there was little strain about accepting this either. He had not, to begin with, entirely given up thoughts of work. He was attracted for some strange reason by the thought of using those felt-tipped markers, known then under their brand-name of 'Magic Markers' which had recently appeared in the shops, and he did attempt some drawings of a sheep's skull that somebody had given him with them. They were not a success, and from then on he did nothing.

He had become strangely religious and, in keeping with his Irishness and presence in Ireland, of course Catholic. He would go to Mass every now and then and would often pop into a church in the middle of the day if he happened to pass one. After a while he possessed a rosary beads. A little while later this had become his dead sister's rosary beads and he kept it twined round one of the posts of his bed. His Catholicism was not supposed to be a conversion, however, for according to the stories he now told, his family and all belonging to him were Catholics.

I was not looking forward to an encounter with Brendan. I had not seen him since the morning he had become famous, more than five years ago. but I had had actual nightmares of him shouting in public houses, his face distorted by hysteria. I was afraid that when we met there would be at the least giant embarrassments, but the first time I saw him was altogether different from any of my imaginings. I was down near the front door of McDaid's one evening, my back towards the length of the pub, when somebody said, 'There's Brendan.' At first I did not turn round, partly through fear of the consequences, but also because I did not want to appear the curious one, or the one who would have to decide about recognition. Then somebody else near me said, 'Well he's making himself comfortable anyway', and I turned around for a quick look. Brendan had lain down on one of the long upholstered seats (which MacBryde called *banquettes*) and he appeared to be already sleeping, his face to the wall. Nobody interfered with him and I decided it was safe to stay in the pub, but a little while later there was a commotion up that end and I turned round again. Two ambulance men who had come in the back door were lifting him up and putting him into a stretcher that they had laid on the floor. Some officious customer had apparently phoned for an ambulance. The wag beside me said, 'Back to the drying shed', and then remarked that although he had seen men thrown out of public houses and carried out of public houses, he had never seen one removed on a stretcher before; but I had caught a glimpse of Brendan's ghastly face and open mouth as they went through the door, and I was not amused.

I first heard of *The Dalkey Archive* shortly after our return from Spain. On the first day I met Myles he told me that he was working on a new book and would like me to read what he had written so far. The idea of a new novel by him was vastly exciting and it was with a feeling of enormous anticipation that I arranged to meet him the following day in Sinnott's of South King Street.

When we met he gave me about twenty thousand words or so of flawless typescript. He told me he was going ahead at the rate of about two thousand words a day and would be finished in a month. He spoke of the book, as he did about all his works, in terms of the jokes it contained.

'Tell me this,' he began. 'Was Saint Augustine a black man or a white man? Of course he could have been a black man because he was born in Africa, but the extraordinary thing is that nobody knows, because the Romans didn't give a damn whether you were or you weren't.' He explained that through a time device, 'something like Wells' (which struck me as an extraordinary comparison) we meet Saint Augustine. 'Everybody will get a hell of a surprise. I can tell you that', he said.

'And did it ever strike you', he went on, 'that James Joyce might still be alive and well somewhere? After all he allegedly died during the war, when a lot of very queer things went on.' He outlined the plot in some detail, a thing which I have noticed novelists are seldom loath to do, though the practice must always make a poet feel that they are taking a dangerous and unnecessary liberty with their muse, whoever she may be. All in all, however, it sounded exciting, with an original form, like his first great book; and it was with high hopes that, after many injunctions about the safety of the manuscript, I took it away.

I was to be sadly disappointed. As I read I had the increasing feeling that this was old stuff, at best rewritten. Much of the circumstance was no longer operative. There were trams and bicycles in the streets; women were not served in lounge bars. There was an idyllic, almost pastoral feeling about the whole thing which suggested Arcadian summers of long ago. Worse still, it was boring. The central joke, De Selby's experiments with time, did not work. The sergeant was mildly humorous padding. The hero's relationship with his girl-friend and the manner of describing it would have been prim and false in 1939. What was I to say about it all?

On consideration I decided that I dared not ask if this was an old work rewritten, for that was definitely not the impression I had been given and to suggest that it read like that would be tantamount to calling him a liar. That it had been rewritten I had little doubt, and this would explain the speed of composition, optimistically transferred to what was to come, as well as perhaps the illusion that he was off to a fresh start. What I had been given brought the story roughly up to De Selby's revelation of his powers and the meeting with Saint Augustine in the cave. There was as yet nothing about James Joyce and there might be better things to come. I even had the feeling that this might be where the old book stopped and the new plunge was about to begin. He might want an assurance that the thing worked before he went on, in which case it would perhaps be wrong to say anything adverse.

Such was my embarrassment, however, that I did nothing for a while. Then I got a note from him addressed to McDaid's: 'Dear Tony, if this reaches you, and not otherwise, please meet me in The Bailey at one o'clock on Thursday.' When we met I could see that he was a bit testy and suspicious because I had kept the typescript so long without saying anything. I had decided, however, that he must be encouraged to go on at all costs, using perhaps, if it was necessary to him, the old stuff as a springboard, and I therefore did my best to praise it. He accepted what I had to say without much comment, but Myles was a sharp fellow and I couldn't help feeling that he smelled a rat.

Shortly afterwards we appeared on the television together, in company with Benedict Kiely and Aidan Higgins. It became apparent almost from the start of the proceedings that Myles was determined to monopolise them and to speak only about his new book. The interviewer said something about *At-Swim-Two-Birds*. 'Juvenilia', declared Myles scornfully, 'mere juvenilia', and then he proceeded to discuss the negritude or otherwise of Saint Augustine. It became apparent also that he was drunk. Somewhere it was decided to cut us off. When it was over Myles turned to Higgins, who had not succeeded in uttering a word of any description throughout the whole affair, and, as one participant to another asked, 'How did that go?'

He had, however, reached his plateau, had been put into good humour by his performance and was in tolerable conversational form. So we went into town and went to McDaid's, where we found Kavanagh. A little to my surprise, Myles elected to join him. It was the time of John Fitzgerald Kennedy's visit to Ireland and there was to be a garden party for him later that week in the grounds of the Presidential residence in the Phoenix Park. Myles broached the subject of this garden party and it was evident that he had something on his mind. After a while I saw what it was: he wanted to find out whether Kavanagh had received an invitation without disclosing whether he had got one himself or not. Kavanagh saw what he was after at about the same time and so the subject came out into the open. Nobody had received an invitation, not even Frank O'Connor, 'the Dean of the Celtic faculty', as Myles called him. There followed condemnations of those 'thooramalauns' who had had the inviting and fanciful imaginings about the sort of 'yobs' who would be there. In fact even the embittered prognostications made that night did not live up to what actually happened. The President of the United States was a little late in coming out on to the lawn to meet the guests. Apparently while they waited for him excitement grew. When he finally did appear almost the entire assemblage rushed forward and, whooping in the accents of Limerick and points west, practically tore the shirt off the poor man's back, so that he had to retreat indoors for another.

If the 'thooramalauns' concerned had refrained from inviting literary men because they feared eccentricities, gaucheries or forthrightness of behaviour, they made a grave miscalculation. The *crème de la crème* behaved worse than literary men could ever have done. Although not perhaps a great President, John Kennedy was undoubtedly in some sort a great man. It would not have mattered much in an assembly of a couple of hundred people who shook his hand, and it matters the less now that all three parties are dead, but it might have cheered Myles or Paddy up a bit to have been invited to such a function, and I recount the story now as evidence of how the writer was regarded as outside social converse altogether in the Ireland of those days.

It must have been on November 22nd of the same year, 1963, after, presumably, he had spent some time in hospital, that I actually met Brendan for the first time since London; and the meeting too was different from anything I had imagined. It was during the holy hour in the back bar of the old Bailey. I was with Thérèse, John Ryan and a fellow who was acting as go-between about a secondhand car I was buying. Brendan came in with a leg-man. I went on talking to my company. Then the waiter brought over a bottle of champagne and some glasses. Simultaneously Brendan joined us. He began to pour and asked me to have some. I refused, saying that I was drinking whiskey, which was true. He immediately ordered a whiskey for me. Then he asked me how I was. I said I was O.K. and how was he himself. He was, it seemed, O.K. too. The conversation flagged a bit. The go-between and I were supposed to go and see the car and he began to agitate for a move. I did not want to leave too soon but I was glad for the time being to have a topic to discuss with someone else. After a while I said we would go, but before we did Brendan called me aside. We stood at the end of the counter and he produced a bundle of notes.

'Are you all right?' he asked. 'For what?' I said.

'For money. For buying this car.' 'Oh, I am', I said 'I'm all right.'

I wasn't really, but for a variety of reasons, some of them I suppose ignoble, that's what I said.

We did not actually buy that car, the go-between and I (we subsequently bought a worse one), but it was after six o'clock when we got back to the Bailey. A waiter told me that my wife and Brendan were upstairs. He had asked her to have a meal with him. The third or fourth bottle of wine had been broached when I joined them, but Brendan was still no more drunk than was customary amongst us all and he had been singing for her. At my request he sang again, several of the old songs that I remembered from what was now the long ago. Then the waiter came over and told us the news had just come in on the radio that John F. Kennedy had been assassinated in Dallas, Texas.

Brendan appeared genuinely shocked by this, as indeed were we all, and after a while he excused himself, paid the bill and left. Next morning I discovered from the newspapers that he must have gone straight to the American Embassy to sign the book of condolences. I thought to myself, 'Well that's show-biz,' but to think this may have been ignoble of me too.

The last two occasions on which I saw Brendan Behan are briefly recorded. Both were in the Bailey. On the first occasion he was leaning against the wall, with his mouth open, speechless and apparently unable to move. He had dried vomit on his lapels and on the uppers of his little shoes. He had two leg-men with him and the odd thing was that they went on drinking cheerfully at the bar, paying no attention to him whatever. From what I gathered he had four or five of these followers all told, layabouts who got taxis for him, ordered drinks, kept him company when no-one else would, dumped him home after he had passed out, or, alternatively, if it suited them better, took him to their own homes instead. One of them lived in a block of council flats and he described to me a week that Brendan had spent there, lying fully dressed in the children's bed, sending out for bottles of whiskey whenever he woke up. 'It was a great party', he said. Brendan of course represented a fair source of income to them all, for, aside from what he parted with out of the goodness of his heart, there was a fair amount to be made even from pocketing the change after buying each drink or paying every taxi. Yet such is human nature that one of them complained to John Ryan that he had given up a good job to look after Brendan Behan.

The next and, as it happens, the last time that I saw him was a day or two later at the counter just inside the door of the same back bar. It was dark inside; you had to duck your head going through the door and come up two steps, so I did not see Brendan until I was standing beside him, ordering myself a drink. He had the remnants of the same dried vomit still on his lapels and on his shoes, so evidently he had not been home since. He made several attempts to say something to me but I could not make out what it was. Sounds, evidently words, came out of his mouth, but they were incomprehensible. Since they were the last words Brendan Behan ever addressed to me I would like to know what they were, but I don't. I finished my drink, said good-bye and left.

Shortly afterwards he died in the Meath Hospital. One of his leg-men claimed afterwards that he had smuggled him in a half-bottle of brandy. If he did, he killed him. Probably he kept the change.

It was about this time that a friend who had been out to see him in the South of France told me of the death of Ralph Cusack. It seemed that his brain had actually exploded. And it was around this time too that I heard, through the newspapers, of the death of Julian Maclaren-Ross.

Before he died he had published in the *London Magazine* a series of portraits of old acquaintances called 'Memoirs of the Forties'. It was his home ground and he was in something very like his old form, that of the author of the story I had long ago liked best, 'Second Lieutenant Lewis', a superb evocation of a brief wartime acquaintance with the poet Alun Lewis. There was the same undertone of irony, the same eye for the small grotesqueries, the same economy of portraiture. To some extent at least the big spender had recouped his losses, the maestro had surprised those who thought he was finished, the rightful heir had frightened the interlopers, the Jacobite exile had had a last revenge. The reviews of the book were lavish, but they took the form of obituaries. Mr. Philip Toynbee described the early stories and the early success, such as it was. After that he said,

'Julian MacLaren-Ross had dropped out of sight.' Perhaps. Out of sight of the larger literary world maybe: even, for so many years, out of sight of his own talent. But the master of disguise was merely in hiding, and, as some of us knew, that was really him all the time, behind the dark glasses.

Myles broke a leg and suffered much discomfort. Then one day I met him in the street. He told me he was looking for a job and was on his way to see a well-known bookseller and publisher who was expanding his publishing activities. We discussed the paucity of jobs in Ireland for people of our ilk. 'I'm skating on very thin ice,' he said. 'All I've got is the pension.' Then he brightened up and said, 'Mind you, between the two sides of the Atlantic I can get a thousand pounds sight unseen for a book.'

A short while later I met him again. I enquired about the leg. 'Did you ever hear of the dominant theme in a symphony?' he asked. 'Well, the leg is no longer the dominant theme.'

Brian O'Nolan died in hospital of cancer of the throat in the summer of 1966. Kavanagh, MacBryde and the retired schoolmaster were together in the back of the church when I arrived, late. I had some trouble in finding a place. Later MacBryde reported to me something that Kavanagh had said. He was capable also of strange generosities behind one's back.

At the graveside there were no words said, except by the priest. As we walked away I said to one of Brian's oldest friends that somebody else should have said something. 'That's right, there should have been a funeral oration', he said. 'I wonder why didn't anybody think of that.'

The flat in Leeson Street where the three retired gentlemen lived had to be given up and Robert went to stay with Leland, sleeping on the couch beside the basement window where Kavanagh had slept before him. One morning I was sitting at our own kitchen table composing an allegedly funny piece for the radio when Leland came round to tell me that Robert had been knocked down by a motor-car on his way home the night before and was dead. His body was in Vincent's Hospital.

I finished my allegedly funny piece, went down to the radio station and recorded it, and then went to Leland's. There were various people there, sitting round the kitchen table, some of them drunk. There was also a policeman who wanted to know about the deceased. Nobody, including the policeman, seemed to have any ideas about what to do.

I knew about Maybole at least and that he had a brother John who had figured in his mythology. Through the Maybole police I got John MacBryde on the telephone. He said that Robert's parents would want his body brought home and that they had burial insurance. I knew that that was what Robert would have wanted himself, for Robert Colquhoun's body had been brought back to Ayrshire also. It was eventually arranged that a friend and I should accompany the body to Scotland, taking it via Belfast to Stranraer, where an undertaker that the MacBrydes had arranged for would take over.

In fact he gave us the slip. Through some misunderstanding the driver of the hearse left Vincent's without waiting for us and Robert had a good hour's start for the border when we followed in Edward Maguire's car. Fast as Edward drove we missed the boat and had to cross to Scotland by air while Robert went by sea. It was a case of 'you take the high road and I'll take the low road, but I'll be in Scotland afore ye.' From Glasgow we had to take a train to, I think, Kilmarnock, and from thence a late bus. When we found the bus-stop it said, 'Maybole and Beyond'. 'So that's where he's gone', said Richard.

The MacBrydes turned out to be splendid people and I met some who had figured in his mythology over the years, including his redoubtable Aunt Maggie. But much of what Robert had told us was fantasy. For one thing, they were all Kirk of Scotland. There was no dead sister and, of course, if there had been she would not have had a rosary beads. There was of course no photograph of Major John MacBride. The last communication his parents had had was a war-time

199

postcard from London and the only evidence of reputation in the outer world they ever saw was a clipping with a photograph of the two Roberts from a war-time *Vogue*. 'They were aye fond of a drop, himself and Robert', said his mother. I agreed they were.

The minister would have put an Irish country priest to shame. He delivered a little homily in the parents' parlour which ended with the words: 'We must not grieve. That sense of form and colour which Robert received from the Lord he has now brought back safe and untarnished to the Lord's keeping.' At the graveside he took as his text: 'Let us now praise famous men and their fathers that begat them.'

It was at the graveside that somebody, whose strong-boned Scots face was familiar, came over and shook hands. 'Would you be John Colquhoun?' I asked. He was. As we left the graveyard he pointed towards Kilmarnock. We could almost see where Robert Colquhoun was buried. 'And Robert Burns is down there,' he said pointing towards Ayr. 'Well they're within roaring distance of each other anyway', I said.

He and I went up town to have a drink. In the first pub a rather obnoxious little man who was evidently acquainted with John came over and would not go away again. Eventually John Colquhoun said; 'Will ye do me a favour?' The obnoxious little man nodded and waited. 'Awa, wi' ye,' roared John. It was very familiar.

In the autumn of that same year, 1966, I went to the University of Montana as Visiting Lecturer in English. The day before I left I went into Sheehan's, which is up the lane from McDaid's. Kavanagh was seated at the counter, all alone. As it happened I was barred in McDaid's, and so, because of some disagreement about cheques, was he. After an instant's hesitation I went to the counter also. 'What'll ye have?' he asked. I said I would have a small Scotch, but he ordered a double. 'So you're off to Amerikay,' he said. I assented. 'And there won't be any conversation now till you come back', he said.

It was not the only such remark he ever made; but as a

general rule I have not recorded them, and only do so now because this was the last conversation we ever had.

He had a swollen and, it appeared, disjointed thumb and had been round in hospital having treatment. I asked him how it had happened.

'Sometimes', he said, 'when I'm lying in bed I don't know whether I'm dreaming or waking. I think things are there in the room, do you know?' I did know, up to a point. 'Well I don't know how in hell it happened but I got some sort of fright and I must have jumped somehow and I fell out of bed on to the floor. I sort of found myself on the floor, do you know, and I hurt my thumb.'

For a long time there had been talk about him getting married; indeed as in some Renaissance court, there was a marriage party and an anti-marriage party among his friends. Though no longer a confidant of his, I was of the marriage party. Apart from the fact that Katherine was an old friend of Thérèse's and an old friend of mine, it was evident that the only thing that could save him now was marriage. Well, he did get married, but it didn't save him. He caught pneumonia in 1968 and, since the old warrior had only one lung left, it proved fatal. I was still in Montana and a friend sent me a cable saying, 'Oh commemorate me where there is water . . .'

May he and the others commemorated in this book enjoy at last, in Elysium or elsewhere, whatever the innermost nature truly seeks. If it be oblivion, so be it.